Instant Pot Duo Crisp Air Fryer Cookbook for Two

Mouthwaterin Crispy and Affordable Recipes for Fast and Healthy

Meals with Your Instant Pot Duo Crisp Air Fryer

Amenas Honew

Table of Contents

Introduction

The pressure cooker in itself had many functions, and with its super quick cooking benefit, people all around the world use it on their stoves. Cooking has become more simple, easier as time has gone by. Wait a few years more, and an innovative multitasking gadget will be introduced, giving healthier living a chance. The air fryer swept the market, and the device found itself trending Now, with great ingenuity, innovation, and creativity, a new kitchen gadget has been released. This device combines the functionality of the pressure cooker and air fryer to give us the ultimate kitchen equipment. This device is capable of replacing all other cooking and heating devices. This device is known as the Instant Pot Duo Crisp Air Fryer.

Except for the obvious pressure cooking and frying functionality, the pressure cooker air fryer combo provides you with six wet cooking functions, including sous vide, steaming slow cooking heating sautéing etc. It also comes with the functions of air fryer crisp cooking such as broiling roasting dehydrating and baking the amount of money you'll save up on this equipment cannot be counted.

These are just some of the benefits listed, but the device is made for ultimate efficiency cooking in the kitchen. With practice and constant use, you will find yourself eating better, staying in the kitchen less, and eating hot food all the time. The hassles of the kitchen are over.

Chapter 1: Instant Pot Duo Crisp Air Fryer Basics

Benefits of Using Instant Pot Duo Crisp Air Fryer

- One-pot cooking

The instant pot series had an amazing functionality that if you cook something in one device, you can transfer the pot into another without pouring out any food. This device goes even further in giving convenience. Now, you can have access to all the various cooking options on the same device. For example, if you are pressure cooking your chicken and you want to add a crispy layer to it on top, you simply need to replace the cooking lid and then press the button from broiling to frying in the same pot; all your cooking is complete. No need to transfer food; the food goes into this pot and then on the plate.

- 10-1 functions

The combination itself provides a lot of options and different settings, but this device gives you more options than an air fryer or a pressure cooker separately could achieve. With the additional functions of dehydration, baking and sous vide, this machine has made much other expensive equipment unnecessary for you.

Heating can easily be done without a microwave, no need for a dehydrator, or sous vide machine. Want to bake out a small batch of cookies quickly? Use the instant pot instead of your bulky oven.

- Efficiency that saves time

Whether you are making a beef broth, tenderizing lentils and beans, or baking

you can do all this in

rather than hours. This saves up your time, money by reducing utility costs, and meals are never delayed. You can place all your ingredients and pre-set your desired cooking time, so the cooking is done when you want it to. The device keeps the food warm as well, so there is no need for reheating You can leave the kitchen when you press start, and it's ok if you forget about it because the device will automatically shut down after the timer is up.

- Simple to use

You may be thinking that with all its functions, the device might be too complicated to use. Nothing can be further from the truth. The device has a friendly user interface, a Smart Program, and labelled buttons that all linked with a bright display. There is no confusion when cooking the multi-functionality comes from changing the lids. The device comes with two, an Air Fryer lid for crisp cooking and a pressure cooker kid for wet cooking

When you place the pressure cooker lid, you can

- Pressure cook
- Sautee
- Sous vide
- Steam
- Slow cook

When you place the air fryer lid, you can

- Air fry
- Roast
- Broil
- Bake
- Dehydrate

Working of Instant Pot Duo Crisp Air Fryer

Pressure Cooking

The device uses the pressure and heat of the steam to raise the temperature to 100°C or 121°F. The pressure cooker setting is the quickest way to cook the food, but you have to be cautious while using it.

The pressure cook setting has 3 stages

1. Preheat stage

When you push the start button after putting in your food and lid, the display will show the message ON, pre-heating the pot. During this time, water inside the inner pot is converted into steam, and pressure starts to build up inside the cooker. The float valve on the top is pushed upwards and seals the pot creating a high-pressure environment. If the air leaks, the press the cancel button and investigates the problem.

2. Cooking stage

After the float valve seals the pot, the pre-heating process finishes after a few minutes. Now, cooking begins, and the timer starts. The display should show the designated pressure, temperature, and time. It will also indicate if the 'Warming' option is on.

3. Depressurize stage

Once the timer is completed, follow the recipe instructions for depressurizing the pot. If the 'Warming' option is on, then the pot depressurizes slowly and keeps the contents warm for 10 hours. If the option is off, then the pot depressurizes quickly.

How to depressurize the instant pot:

You must never open the lid while the float valve is sealed. Only open after the pressure has been released.

When the cooking is done, the float value comes down to the lid level. This indicates that the pot has been completely depressurized. Different foods need to be depressurized at different timings, so follow the recipe for the best results. If you're cooking something that expands, for example, pasta, chili, beans, lentils, don't push the quick release (QR) bottom on top of the lid. Leave it in seal position until it comes down to the lid level by itself. This could take 10 to 15 minutes.

For other ingredients that are not high in starch and don't expand, you can use the (QR) button. After cooking press on the button until it reaches the lid level and allows continuous air release. Stay away from the hot air coming from the vent.

Air Frying

Air frying is an extremely quick and healthy way of making your everyday delightful snacks. Tasty food doesn't need to be greasy, deep-fried, or be filled with fat. By air frying

you can make deep-fry dishes by using only a splash of oil.

The fryer setting works best for shrimps, French fries, chicken wings, and frozen fries. The cook ranges from 2 to 10

at 400°F or 212°C temperature.

Firstly, put the food inside the inner pot or the oven-safe air fryer basket. Both of them work well. If you are using an accessory, then first clean and proper place it inside. Connect your device to a 120 V electric source, the display will show 'OFF,' and the cooker will be in standby mode. Place the pot inside the cooker base and close the air fryer lid on top. Ensure that the air fryer's handles align with the pot's until it makes a jingle sound. This ensures that the device is properly closed. Press the button Air fry on the device and use Smart Program to adjust the time and temperature.

Now, press on the start button, which will begin the pre-heating process. When the display shifts from 'ON' to the timer, that means the pre-heat stage is completed, and cooking has begun.

Between the cookin

the display will show 'Turn Food.' You have to open the lid, turn the food, and close the lid back again at this stage. The indicator will stop after 10 seconds, and the timer will continue forward if you don't interact with the device at this moment. Also, don't worry if you are taking a long time to flip your food. The cooker goes into standby after 3

of opening the lid. Place the lid over the protective pad that comes with the device.

When the cooking ends, the device will let you know with a beep and the display will show 'END'.

Cleaning and Maintenance and Tips

- Always wash your Instant Pot Duo Crisp Air Fryer after every use.
- Don't immediately use it after cleaning
- let the device dry, and then proceed to use it.
- When done cooking
- remove the power cord and let it sit for a few
- until it completely cools down. Then, clean the device.

Cleaning Instructions:

Different parts of the device need to be cleaned differently. The parts and their preferred cleaning method and maintenance are listed below

1. Accessories

These include Multifunctional Rack, Condensation Collector, Air Fryer Basket, Air Fryer Basket Base, Dehydration/Broiling tray.

Instructions:

- Don't use harsh chemicals or detergents
- Rinse the collector thoroughly
- You can use cooking spray and small amounts of oil on trays and baskets
- Place on the top rack in the dishwasher
- Disassemble the basket for thorough cleaning
- You can hand wash as well

2. Pressure cooker lid and its parts

Instructions:

- Use mild hot water and soap to clean the lid and allow drying by dry air.
- Place it on the top rack of the dishwasher
- After removing the valve and anti-block shield, properly rinse the steam release pipe to prevent clogging
- Disassemble the lid parts before cleaning

- Drain soapy water from the lid by rotating it under a water tap like a steering wheel.
- Place the lid upside on the pot for drying
- To prevent odor from developing
- place one cup water, one cup white vinegar in the pot and set it on "pressure cook" for 5-10 minutes.

3. Inner pot

Instructions:

- Fully dry it before placing it inside the pot
- For hard stains, use a vinegar-soaked sponge and scrubbing method to clean the pot
- You can hand wash it or place it in the dishwasher

4. Air fryer lid

Instructions:

- Turn it off after use and let it sit until it's completely cooled
- Only use a dampened cloth and NOT use water near the heating element
- Don't place it in water or rinse
- Don't remove element cover

5. Power cord

Instructions:

- Don't rinse or place it underwater
- Only remove grease and particles off with a dampened cloth

6. Cooker base

Instructions:

- Rub a slightly dampened cloth on the anterior surface and condensation rim
- Don't rinse or place it underwater

Chapter 2: 30-Day Meal Plan

Day 1

Breakfast: Yogurt

Lunch: Chicken Wings

Dinner: Herbed Rotisserie Chicken

Dessert: Apple Cobbler

Day 2

Breakfast: Banana Bread

Lunch: Pork Chops

Dinner: Pork Tenderloin

Dessert: Apple Chips

Day 3

Breakfast: Sausage and Onions

Lunch: Savory Potato Bake

Dinner: Crispy Tofu

Dessert: Peach Cobbler

Day 4

Breakfast: Sausages

Lunch: Sous Vide Steak

Dinner: Beef Stew

Dessert: Brownies

Day 5

Breakfast: Breakfast Casserole

Lunch: Salmon with Dill Sauce

Dinner: Shrimp Fried Rice

Dessert: Cherry Cake

Day 6

Breakfast: Broccoli Sous Vide Egg Bites

Lunch: Chicken Casserole

Dinner: Pad Thai with Chicken Fried Rice

Dessert: Lemon Pudding Cups

Day 7

Breakfast: Bacon and Gruyere Egg Bites

Lunch: Pot Roast

Dinner: Burnt Ends

Dessert: Sweet Apples

Day 8

Breakfast: Scrambled Eggs

Lunch: Baked Potatoes

Dinner: Cauliflower Wings

Dessert: Fudgy Chocolate Cake

Day 9

Breakfast: Omelet

Lunch: Beef Brisket

Dinner: Cod with Lemon

Dessert: Custard

Day 10

Breakfast: Bacon

Lunch: Tuna Steaks

Dinner: Parmesan Roast Chicken

Dessert: Rice Pudding

Day 11

Breakfast: Yogurt

Lunch: Whole Chicken

Dinner: BBQ Baby Back Ribs

Dessert: Apple Cobbler

Day 12

Breakfast: Banana Bread

Lunch: Pork Carnitas

Dinner: Loaded Potato Soup

Dessert: Apple Chips

Day 13

Breakfast: Sausage and Onions

Lunch: Spicy Potato Halves

Dinner: Butter Shrimps

Dessert: Peach Cobbler

Day 14

Breakfast: Sausages

Lunch: Meatloaf

Dinner: Chicken Teriyaki

Dessert: Brownies

Day 15

Breakfast: Breakfast Casserole

Lunch: Lemon Pepper Salmon

Dinner: Country Style Ribs

Dessert: Cherry Cake

Day 16

Breakfast: Broccoli Sous Vide Egg Bites

Lunch: Barbecue Chicken

Dinner: Fish Cakes

Dessert: Lemon Pudding Cups

Day 17

Breakfast: Bacon and Gruyere Egg Bites

Lunch: Pizza Pasta

Dinner: Chicken Tenders

Dessert: Sweet Apples

Day 18

Breakfast: Scrambled Eggs

Lunch: Spare Ribs

Dinner: Honey Garlic Ribs

Dessert: Fudgy Chocolate Cake

Day 19

Breakfast: Omelet

Lunch: Ranch Fish

Dinner: Zucchini and Tomato Mélange

Dessert: Custard

Day 20

Breakfast: Bacon

Lunch: Roasted Artichokes

Dinner: Fish Tacos

Dessert: Rice Pudding

Day 21

Breakfast: Yogurt

Lunch: Halibut with Creamy Cheese Sauce

Dinner: Honey Garlic Chicken and
Vegetables

Dessert: Apple Cobbler

Day 22

Breakfast: Banana Bread

Lunch: Chicken and Broccoli Stir-Fry

Dinner: Crispy Tofu

Dessert: Apple Chips

Day 23

Breakfast: Sausage and Onions

Lunch: Pulled Pork

Dinner: Chicken Wings

Dessert: Peach Cobbler

Day 24

Breakfast: Sausages

Lunch: Spaghetti

Dinner: Pork Chops

Dessert: Brownies

Day 25

Breakfast: Breakfast Casserole

Lunch: Pad Thai with Chicken Fried Rice

Dinner: Savory Potato Bake

Dessert: Cherry Cake

Day 26

Breakfast: Broccoli Sous Vide Egg Bites

Lunch: Burnt Ends

Dinner: Sous Vide Steak

Dessert: Lemon Pudding Cups

Day 27

Breakfast: Bacon and Gruyere Egg Bites

Lunch: Cauliflower Wings

Dinner: Salmon with Dill Sauce

Dessert: Sweet Apples

Day 28

Breakfast: Scrambled Eggs

Lunch: Cod with Lemon

Dinner: Chicken Casserole

Dessert: Fudgy Chocolate Cake

Day 29

Breakfast: Omelet

Lunch: Parmesan Roast Chicken

Dinner: Pot Roast

Dessert: Custard

Day 30

Breakfast: Bacon

Lunch: BBQ Baby Back Ribs

Dinner: Baked Potatoes

Dessert: Rice Pudding

Chapter 3: Breakfast

Yogurt

Preparation time: 5 minutes
Cooking time: 9 hours
Servings: 2

Ingredients:

- ½ tablespoon yogurt, with active cultures
- 3.5 ounces condensed milk, unsweetened
- 4 cups milk, ultra-pasteurized

Method:

1. Turn on the Instant Pot Duo Crisp Air Fryer, add the ingredients in the inner pot, and then whisk well until very smooth.
2. Shut the instant pot with the pressure cooker lid, select the "sous vide" option, press +/- buttons to adjust the cooking temperature to 113 degrees F and cooking time to 9 hours, and then press the start button.
3. When the instant pot, do a quick pressure release, transfer the yogurt to a large bowl and then refrigerate for a minimum of 4 hours until chilled.
4. Serve straight away.

Nutrition Value:

- Calories: 128.4
- Fat: 3.1
- Carbs: 14.4
- Protein: 10.7
- Fiber: 0 g

Banana Bread

Preparation time: 10 minutes
Cooking time: 25 minutes
Servings: 2

Ingredients:

- 1 banana, mashed
- ½ cup all-purpose flour
- 1/3 teaspoon baking soda
- 1/3 teaspoon baking powder
- 1/8 teaspoon salt
- 1/8 teaspoon ground cinnamon
- 1/3 tablespoon brown sugar
- ¼ cup of sugar
- 1/3 teaspoon vanilla extract, unsweetened
- 2 tablespoons melted butter
- 1/3 of eg
- at room temperature, whisked
- 1 cup of water

Method:

1. Turn on the Instant Pot Duo Crisp Air Fryer and then let it preheat.
2. Meanwhile, take a 7-inch springform pan and then grease it with some butter.
3. Take a large bowl, place the mashed bananas in it, add remaining ingredients except for brown sugar and water, and then whisk until incorporated and smooth batter comes together.
4. Spoon the batter into the springform pan, smooth the top, sprinkle brown sugar on top, and then cover the top of the pan tightly with foil.
5. Pour the water into the inner pot, insert the steam rack, and then place the prepared pan on top.
6. Shut the instant pot with the pressure cooker lid, select the "pressure cook" option, press +/- buttons to adjust the cooking time to 25 minutes, select the high-pressure settin
7. and then press the start button.
8. When the instant pot, do natural pressure release for 20
9. and then check the firmness of the cake by inserting a toothpick; it should come out clean.
10. Remove the springform pan from the pot, let it cool for 15 minutes, then take the cake out and cool completely on the wire rack.
11. Cut the cake into slices and then serve.

Nutrition Value:

- Calories: 164.4
- Fat: 7.1

- Carbs: 23.6
- Protein: 2.7
- Fiber: 0.6 g

Sausage and Onions

Preparation time: 5 minutes
Cooking time: 20 minutes
Servings: 2

Ingredients:

- 10 ounces smoked sausages, sliced
- 1 medium white onion, peeled, diced
- 1 tablespoon olive oil
- ¾ teaspoon salt
- ½ teaspoon ground black pepper

Method:

1. Turn on the Instant Pot Duo Crisp Air Fryer and then press the sauté button.
2. Add oil and when hot, add onion and then cook for 3 to 5
3. until onions turn tender.
4. Stir in salt and black pepper, transfer the cooked onions to the air fryer basket and then add sausages.
5. Insert the fryer basket into the instant pot, shut with the air fryer lid, select the "air fryer" option, press +/- buttons to adjust the cooking temperature to 400 degrees F, and cooking time to 15 minutes, and then press the start button.
6. Cook the onions and sausages until nicely brown, stirring halfway, and then serve.

Nutrition Value:

- Calories: 754
- Fat: 69
- Carbs: 5
- Protein: 28
- Fiber: 0 g

Sausages

Preparation time: 5 minutes
Cooking time: 15 minutes

Servings: 2

Ingredients:

- 2 breakfast sausages
- 1 cup water

Method:

1. Turn on the Instant Pot Duo Crisp Air Fryer, pour the water into the inner pot, insert the air fryer basket in it and then spray with oil.
2. Arrange the sausage links into the air fryer basket, and then shut with the pressure cooker lid.
3. Select the "pressure cook" option, select the high pressure, press +/- buttons to adjust the cooking time to 5 minutes, and press the start button.
4. When done, do the quick pressure release, uncover the lid and then spray with oil.
5. Cover the instant pot with the air fryer lid, select the "air fryer" option, press +/- buttons to adjust the cooking temperature to 400 degrees F, and cooking time to 8 minutes.
6. Continue cooking until sausages turn nicely brown on all sides, turning halfway, and then serve.

Nutrition Value:

- Calories: 258
- Fat: 23
- Carbs: 1
- Protein: 13
- Fiber: 0 g

Breakfast Casserole

Preparation time: 5 minutes
Cooking time: 2 hours and 50 minutes
Servings: 2

Ingredients:

- ½ tablespoon butter, salted
- ¼ pound ham, cubed
- ¼ of a medium white onion, peeled, diced
- ¼ pound potatoes, peeled, diced

- ¼ cup heavy whipping cream
- 3 eggs
- 3.2 ounces grated cheddar cheese

Method:

1. Turn on the Instant Pot Duo Crisp Air Fryer, press the sauté button, add butter into the inner pot and then let it melt.
2. Add onion, cook for 3
3. or until sauté and then stir in potatoes.
4. Crack the eggs in a medium bowl and then whisk until blended.
5. When the onions have cooked, press the keep warm/cancel button, pour the egg mixture over the onions, add ham, cheese, and heavy cream and then stir until combined.
6. Shut the instant pot with the pressure cooker lid, select the "slow cooker" option, select the low heat setting
7. press +/- buttons to adjust the cooking time to 2 hours and 45 minutes, and then press the start button.
8. Serve straight away.

Nutrition Value:

- Calories: 523
- Fat: 40
- Carbs: 8
- Protein: 31
- Fiber: 1 g

Broccoli Sous Vide Egg Bites

Preparation time: 10 minutes
Cooking time: 10 minutes
Servings: 2

Ingredients:

- 2 tablespoons chopped and cooked broccoli
- 3 tablespoons shredded cheddar cheese
- 3 tablespoons cottage cheese

- 1 ½ egg
- 1 cup of water

Method:

1. Turn on the Instant Pot Duo Crisp Air Fryer, pour water into the inner pot, and then insert the steamer rack in it.
2. Place all the ingredients in a medium bowl, whisk until combined, and then divide the batter evenly among two silicone cups.
3. Cover the cups with foil, arrange them on the steamer rack, and then shut the instant pot with the pressure cooker lid.
4. Select the "steam" option, press +/- buttons to adjust the time to 10 minutes, and then press the start button.
5. When done, do a natural pressure release, remove the silicone muffin cups, uncover them, and then let the egg bite rest for 5 minutes.
6. Remove the egg bites from the cups and then serve.

Nutrition Value:

- Calories: 82
- Fat: 5
- Carbs: 1
- Protein: 6
- Fiber: 0.3 g

Bacon and Gruyere Egg Bites

Preparation time: 5 minutes
Cooking time: 10 minutes
Servings: 2

Ingredients:

- 2 ¼ tablespoons chopped cooked bacon
- 1/7 tablespoon chopped parsley
- 1/14 teaspoon garlic powder
- 1/14 teaspoon salt
- 1/14 teaspoon ground black pepper
- 2 ¼ tablespoons shredded Gruyere cheese
- 1 ¼ egg
- 1 tablespoon cottage cheese
- 1/3 cup water

Method:

1. Turn on the Instant Pot Duo Crisp Air Fryer, pour water into the inner pot, and then insert the steamer rack in it.
2. Place all the ingredients in a medium bowl, whisk until combined, and then divide the batter evenly among two silicone cups.
3. Cover the cups with foil, arrange them on the steamer rack, and then shut the instant pot with the pressure cooker lid.
4. Select the "steam" option, press +/- buttons to adjust the time to 10 minutes, and then press the start button.
5. When done, do a natural pressure release for 5 minutes, do a quick pressure release, remove the silicone muffin cups, uncover them, and then let the egg bite rest for 5 minutes.
6. Remove the egg bites from the cups and then serve.

Nutrition Value:

- Calories: 300
- Fat: 20
- Carbs: 9
- Protein: 19
- Fiber: 0 g

Scrambled Eggs

Preparation time: 5 minutes
Cooking time: 5 minutes
Servings: 2

Ingredients:

- ¼ teaspoon salt
- ½ teaspoon allspice mix
- ¼ teaspoon ground black pepper
- 2 tablespoons butter, unsalted
- 4 eggs
- 2 tablespoons shredded cheddar cheese
- 4 tablespoons milk

Method:

1. Turn on the Instant Pot Duo Crisp Air Fryer, press the sauté button, add butter into the inner pot and then let it melt.
2. Crack eggs in a medium bowl, add remaining ingredients and then whisk until blended.
3. Pour the egg mixture into the inner pot, stir and then cook for 3 to 5
4. until eggs have scrambled to the desired level.
5. Serve straight away.

Nutrition Value:

- Calories: 80
- Fat: 5
- Carbs: 1.2
- Protein: 7.1
- Fiber: 0 g

Omelet

Preparation time: 5 minutes
Cooking time: 8 minutes
Servings: 2

Ingredients:

- 2 tablespoons chopped red bell pepper
- 1/8 teaspoon salt
- 2 tablespoons chopped green onions
- 2 tablespoons chopped ham
- 1 teaspoon breakfast seasoning
- 2 tablespoons chopped mushroom
- 2 eggs
- ¼ cup shredded cheddar cheese
- ¼ cup whole milk

Method:

1. Crack the eggs in a medium bowl, add remaining ingredients except for breakfast seasoning and cheese and then whisk until well mixed.
2. Take a 6-by-3 inches baking pan, grease it with oil and then pour the mixture in it.
3. Turn on the Instant Pot Duo Crisp Air Fryer, insert the air fryer basket and then place the prepared pan in it.

4. Shut the instant pot with the air fryer lid, select the "air fryer" option, press +/- buttons to adjust the cooking temperature to 350 degrees F and cooking time to 4 minutes, and then press the start button.
5. Sprinkle the breakfast seasoning on top of omelet, sprinkle cheese over the top and then continue cooking for 4 minutes.
6. When done, transfer the omelet to a plate and then serve.

Nutrition Value:

- Calories: 160.5
- Fat: 11.3
- Carbs: 5.1
- Protein: 9.2
- Fiber: 0.7 g

Bacon

Preparation time: 5 minutes
Cooking time: 10 minutes
Servings: 2

Ingredients:

- ¼ pound bacon, thick cut

Method:

1. Turn on the Instant Pot Duo Crisp Air Fryer, insert the air-fryer basket, and then grease it with oil.
2. Arrange the bacon into the air fryer basket in a single layer, and then shut the instant pot with the air fryer lid.
3. Select the "air fryer" option, press +/- buttons to adjust the cooking temperature to 400 degrees F and cooking time to 10 minutes, and then press the start button.
4. While cooking the bacon, turn it halfway through and then cook it until crisp and golden brown.
5. Serve straight away.

Nutrition Value:

- Calories: 46
- Fat: 3.6
- Carbs: 0.1

- Protein: 3.1
- Fiber: 0 g

Chapter 4: Poultry

Chicken Wings

Preparation time: 10 minutes
Cooking time: 22 minutes
Servings: 2

Ingredients:

- 4 chicken wings
- 1/8 teaspoon garlic powder
- 1/8 teaspoon cayenne pepper
- ¼ teaspoon salt
- ¼ teaspoon ground black pepper
- 3 tablespoons red hot sauce
- 1/3 tablespoon white vinegar
- 1/8 teaspoon Worcestershire sauce
- 1 tablespoon butter, unsalted
- ½ tablespoon olive oil
- 1/3 cup chicken broth

Method:

1. Turn on the Instant Pot Duo Crisp Air Fryer, pour the broth into the inner pot, insert the air fryer basket and then arrange the chicken wings in it.
2. Shut the instant pot with the pressure cooker lid, select the "pressure cook" option, select the high pressure, press +/- buttons to adjust the cooking time to 12 minutes, and then press the start button.
3. Meanwhile, prepare the sauce and for this, take a small saucepan, place it over medium-high heat, add remaining ingredients except for salt and black pepper and then whisk until combined.
4. Cook the sauce for 3 to 5
5. until it begins to bubble, remove the pan from heat, and then set it aside until required; keep it hot.
6. When the instant pot beeps, do a quick pressure release, take out the air fryer basket and drain the inner pot.
7. Spray the oil over the chicken wings on both sides, sprinkle with salt and black pepper and then return the air fryer basket into the instant pot.

8. Shut the instant pot with air fryer lid, press +/- buttons to adjust the cooking temperature to 400 degrees F and cooking time to 10 minutes, and then press the start button.

9. Turn the chicken wings halfway, and when done, brush the sauce over the chicken wings until thoroughly coated and then serve.

Nutrition Value:

- Calories: 463
- Fat: 40
- Carbs: 10

- Protein: 16
- Fiber: 1 g

Chicken Casserole

Preparation time: 10 minutes
Cooking time: 10 minutes
Servings: 2

Ingredients:

- 1 stalk of celery, chopped
- 1/3 packet of French's onions
- 1 cup of shredded cooked chicken
- 2 tablespoons chopped broccoli florets
- 2 tablespoons frozen peas
- ¼ pf a medium white onion, chopped
- ¼ teaspoon garlic powder

- ¼ cup chopped carrots
- ¼ teaspoon salt
- ¼ teaspoon ground black pepper
- 4 ounces egg noodles
- 1 tablespoon sour cream
- 1/3 cup shredded cheddar cheese
- 1 ½ cup chicken broth
- ½ cup cream of chicken and mushroom soup

Method:

1. Turn on the Instant Pot Duo Crisp Air Fryer, add chicken and all the vegetables, stir in garlic powder, salt, and black pepper, and then pour in the broth.

2. Stir until mixed, add the egg noodles, and then stir until just mixed.

3. Shut the instant pot with the pressure cooker lid, select the "pressure cook" option, select the high heat setting

4. press +/- buttons to adjust the cooking time to 4 minutes, and then press the start button.

5. When the instant pot beeps, do a quick pressure release, add soup, sour cream, and 1/4th of the French onions and then stir until mixed.

6. Sprinkle the remaining French onions on top, and then shut the instant pot with the air fryer lid.

7. Press the air fryer option, press +/- buttons to adjust the cooking temperature to 400 degrees F, press +/- buttons to adjust the cooking time to 5 minutes, and then press the start button.

8. Cook the casserole until the top turn golden brown, and then serve.

Nutrition Value:

- Calories: 300
- Fat: 17
- Carbs: 17
- Protein: 2
- Fiber: 2 g

Whole Chicken

Preparation time: 10 minutes
Cooking time: 35 minutes
Servings: 2

Ingredients:

- 1 whole chicken, cleaned, rinsed
- 1 teaspoon garlic powder
- 1 teaspoon onion powder
- 1 teaspoon Italian seasoning
- 1 teaspoon paprika
- 2 tablespoon steak seasoning
- 2 tablespoons olive oil
- 1 ½ cup chicken broth

Method:

1. Prepare the chicken and for this, take a small bowl, place the Italian seasoning and steak seasoning in it, stir until mixed, and then rub some of this mixture all over the chicken.
2. Turn on the Instant Pot Duo Crisp Air Fryer, pour the chicken broth into the inner pot, and then insert the air fryer basket in it.
3. Arrange the prepared chicken in it, shut the instant pot with the pressure cooker lid, select the "pressure cook" option, select the high-pressure setting
4. press +/- buttons to adjust the cooking time to 25 minutes, and then press the start button.
5. When the instant pot beep, do a natural pressure release, open the instant pot and then spray the chicken with oil.
6. Sprinkle the remaining seasoning mixture all over the chicken until coated, shut the instant pot with the lid, select the "air fryer" option, and then air-fry it for 10
7. at 400 degrees F.
8. Then turn the chicken, season it with the remaining seasoning mixture and then continue cooking for 10
9. or more until thoroughly cooked.
10. When done, let the chicken rest for 10 minutes, then carve it into slices and serve.

Nutrition Value:

- Calories: 441
- Fat: 28
- Carbs: 4
- Protein: 42
- Fiber: 1 g

Herbed Rotisserie Chicken

Preparation time: 10 minutes
Cooking time: 1 hour
Servings: 2

Ingredients:

- 1 whole chicken, cleaned, rinsed
- 1 ½ teaspoon salt
- 1 teaspoon Italian seasoning
- 1 teaspoon ground black pepper

- 2 teaspoons onion powder
- 2 teaspoons garlic powder
- 1 teaspoon paprika
- 1 tablespoon dried thyme
- 2 tablespoons olive oil

Method:

1. Turn on the Instant Pot Duo Crisp Air Fryer and then insert the air fryer basket.
2. Tie the legs, thighs, and wings of the chicken, brush it with oil and then season with salt and black pepper.
3. Take a small bowl, place remaining ingredients in it, stir until mixed, and then rub this mixture all over the chicken.
4. Arrange the chicken into the air fryer basket, shut the instant pot with the air fryer lid, select the "air fryer" option, press +/- buttons to adjust the cooking temperature to 380 degrees F, and cooking time to 1 hour, and then press the start button.
5. When done, wrap the chicken in foil, let it rest for 10 minutes, and then carve it into pieces.
6. Serve straight away.

Nutrition Value:

- Calories: 495
- Fat: 34
- Carbs: 3
- Protein: 41
- Fiber: 1 g

Pad Thai with Chicken Fried Rice

Preparation time: 10 minutes
Cooking time: 30 minutes
Servings: 2

Ingredients:

- ½ package of Pad Thai rice noodles
- 1 chicken breasts, cut into thin pieces
- 2 cups cooked rice
- ½ of a can of sliced water chestnuts, drained
- ½ cup sliced shiitake mushroom
- ½ cup frozen peas

- 1 carrot, peeled, sliced
- ½ of a medium onion, peeled, sliced
- ½ tablespoon minced garlic
- ½ teaspoon salt
- ½ teaspoon ground black pepper
- 1/8 teaspoon red chili flakes
- ½ tablespoon soy sauce
- 1 ½ tablespoon olive oil
- 2 tablespoons chicken broth
- 2 cups of water

For the Sauce:

- ½ teaspoon minced garlic
- 1/8 teaspoon ground black pepper
- 1 tablespoon brown sugar
- 1 tablespoon lime juice
- ½ cup chicken broth
- 2 tablespoons soy sauce
- ¼ cup of water

Method:

1. Take a shallow dish, place the chicken pieces in it, season with salt and black pepper and then toss until combined.
2. Turn on the Instant Pot Duo Crisp Air Fryer, select the sauté option, and then let it heat.
3. Add all the ingredients for the sauce into the inner pot, whisk until combined, bring the sauce to a simmer and then cook until thickened slightly.
4. When done, transfer the sauce to a bowl and set aside until required.
5. Rinse the inner pot, return it to the instant pot, pour in water, and add noodles.
6. Shut the instant pot with the pressure cooker lid, select the "pressure cook" option, select the high-pressure setting
7. press +/- buttons to adjust the cooking time to 3 minutes and press the start button.
8. When done, do a quick pressure release and then transfer noodles to a bowl.
9. Select the sauté option, add oil into the inner pot, and then let it heat.
10. Add onion, cook for 2 minutes, add seasoned chicken slices, and then cook for 5
11. or more until thoroughly cooked and golden brown.
12. Add all the vegetables, stir in red chili flakes and soy sauce, pour in the chicken broth, and then stir fry for 5 minutes.
13. Add cooked rice, stir in garlic until combined, and then continue cooking for 5
14. until rice turns golden brown.

15. Add the cooked noodles, stir until mixed, and then cook for 2
16. until hot.
17. Serve straight away.

Nutrition Value:

- Calories: 667
- Fat: 13
- Carbs: 109
- Protein: 27
- Fiber: 4 g

Parmesan Roast Chicken

Preparation time: 10 minutes
Cooking time: 45 minutes
Servings: 2

Ingredients:

- 1 ½ pound chicken
- 1 lemon, juiced, zested
- 1 teaspoon red pepper flakes
- 1 ½ teaspoon salt
- 1 teaspoon chopped rosemary
- 1 ½ teaspoon ground black pepper
- 2 sprigs of rosemary
- 3 tablespoons grated parmesan cheese
- 2 tablespoons olive oil
- 2 cups chicken broth

Method:

1. Take a small bowl, place the lemon zest in it, add salt, black pepper, red pepper flakes, and rosemary, and then stir until combined.
2. Rub this mixture all over the chicken and then stuff rosemary sprigs into its cavity.
3. Turn on the Instant Pot Duo Crisp Air Fryer, pour in the chicken broth, and then place the prepared chicken in it.
4. Shut the instant pot with the pressure cooker lid, select the "pressure cook" option, select the high-pressure setting
5. press +/- buttons to adjust the cooking time to 20 minutes and press the start button.

6. When done, do a quick pressure release, transfer chicken to a plate and then drain the inner pot.
7. Return the inner pot into the instant pot, insert the air fryer basket, coat the chicken with oil and then place it into the basket.
8. Shut the instant pot with the air fryer basket, select the "air fryer" option, press +/- buttons to adjust the cooking temperature to 400 degrees F, press +/- buttons to adjust the cooking time to 25 minutes.
9. When the chicken has cooked halfway, sprinkle cheese over the chicken and then continue cooking or until done.
10. When the chicken has cooked, let it rest for 10 minutes, drizzle the lemon juice over the chicken and then cut it into pieces.
11. Serve straight away.

Nutrition Value:

- Calories: 313.3
- Fat: 15
- Carbs: 17

- Protein: 44.3
- Fiber: 1.3 g

Chicken Teriyaki

Preparation time: 10 minutes
Cooking time: 1hour and 10 minutes
Servings: 2

Ingredients:

- 2 chicken thighs, bone-in, skin on

For the Marinade:

- ¼ teaspoon ginger powder
- 1 ½ tablespoon erythritol
- ¼ teaspoon xanthan gum

- ¼ cup chicken broth

- 1 tablespoon dry sake
- ¼ cup of soy sauce
- ½ teaspoon sesame oil

Method:

1. Take a small bowl, place all the ingredients for the marinade, and then stir until combined.
2. Pour the marinade into a large plastic ba
3. add chicken thighs in it, seal the bag making sure there is no air in it, and then turn it upside down until coated.
4. Place the chicken bag into the inner pot, pour in water until the bag has completely submerged.
5. Turn on the Instant Pot Duo Crisp Air Fryer, shut the instant pot with the pressure cooker lid, select the "sous vide" option, press +/- buttons to adjust the cooking temperature to 145 degrees F and cooking time to 55 minutes, and then press the start button.
6. When done, remove the chicken bag from the inner pot and then drain the inner pot.
7. Insert the air fryer basket in it, spread the chicken into the basket in a single layer, and then shut with the air fryer lid, reserving the marinade.
8. Select the "air fryer" option, press +/- buttons to adjust the cooking temperature to 400 degrees F and cooking time to 5 minutes, and then press the start button.
9. When done, transfer chicken to a plate and remove the air fryer basket.
10. Pour the reserved marinade into the inner pot, pour in the chicken broth, press the sauté button, and then cook the sauce or thicken to the desired level.
11. Drizzle the sauce over the chicken and then serve.

Nutrition Value:

- Calories: 510
- Fat: 12.2
- Carbs: 56.7
- Protein: 42.7
- Fiber: 3.6 g

Barbecue Chicken

Preparation time: 10 minutes
Cooking time: 21 minutes
Servings: 2

Ingredients:

- 1 ½ pound chicken, cut into pieces
- ½ teaspoon garlic powder
- ½ teaspoon salt
- ½ teaspoon paprika
- ½ cup barbecue sauce

Method:

1. Take a large bowl, place the chicken pieces in it, add garlic powder, salt, and paprika and then toss until coated.
2. Turn on the Instant Pot Duo Crisp Air Fryer, insert the fryer basket, grease it with oil, and then arrange the chicken in it.
3. Shut the instant pot with the air fryer lid, select the "air fryer" option, press +/- buttons to adjust the cooking temperature to 375 degrees F and cooking time to 18 minutes, and then press the start button.
4. When done, transfer chicken pieces to a plate, brush them with BBQ sauce, and then return them into the air fryer basket.
5. Shut the instant pot with the air fryer lid, select the "air fryer" option, press +/- buttons to adjust the cooking temperature to 350 degrees F and cooking time to 3 minutes, and then press the start button.
6. Serve straight away.

Nutrition Value:

- Calories: 182
- Fat: 5
- Carbs: 24.8
- Protein: 9
- Fiber: 5.6 g

Chicken and Broccoli Stir-Fry

Preparation time: 10 minutes
Cooking time: 20 minutes
Servings: 2

Ingredients:

- ½ pound chicken breast, cut into bite-size pieces
- ¼ of a medium onion, peeled, sliced
- 1 cup broccoli florets
- ¼ teaspoon salt
- ½ teaspoon ground black pepper

For the Marinade:

- ¼ teaspoon garlic powder
- ½ tablespoon grated ginger
- ½ tablespoon soy sauce
- 1 teaspoon hot sauce
- 1 teaspoon apple cider vinegar
- ½ teaspoon sesame oil
- 1 tablespoon olive oil

Method:

1. Take a large bowl, place chicken pieces in it, add onion and broccoli, and then toss until combined.
2. Prepare the marinade and for this, take a small bowl, place all of its ingredients in it and then whisk until combined.
3. Drizzle the marinade over the chicken and vegetables, toss until coated, and let it rest for 10 minutes.
4. Then turn on the Instant Pot Duo Crisp Air Fryer, insert the fryer basket, and then grease it with oil.
5. Add the marinated chicken and vegetables into the fryer basket, and then shut the instant pot with the air fryer lid.
6. Select the "air fryer" option, press +/- buttons to adjust the cooking temperature to 380 degrees F and cooking time to 20 minutes, and then press the start button.
7. Toss the chicken and vegetables halfway through, and when done, season with salt and black pepper.
8. Serve straight away.

Nutrition Value:

- Calories: 191
- Fat: 7
- Carbs: 4
- Protein: 25
- Fiber: 1 g

Chicken Tenders

Preparation time: 10 minutes
Cooking time: 25 minutes
Servings: 2

Ingredients:

- ¾ pound chicken tenders
- 1 teaspoon salt
- ½ teaspoon ground black pepper
- ½ teaspoon garlic powder
- ½ teaspoon dried oregano
- ½ tablespoon Italian seasoning
- ¼ teaspoon dried thyme
- ½ tablespoon paprika
- ¼ teaspoon mustard powder
- ¼ cup grated parmesan cheese

Method:

1. Prepare the chicken and for this, season them with salt and black pepper until coated.
2. Take a shallow dish, place remaining ingredients in it, stir until combined, and then dredge the chicken tenders in it until well coated.
3. Turn on the Instant Pot Duo Crisp Air Fryer, insert the air fryer basket, and then spray with oil.
4. Arrange the chicken tender into the basket in a single layer, spray with oil, and then shut the instant pot with the air fryer lid.
5. Select the "air fryer" option, press +/- buttons to adjust the cooking temperature to 385 degrees F and cooking time to 12 minutes, and then press the start button.
6. Flip the chicken tenders halfway and when done, transfer chicken tenders to a plate and then repeat with the remaining chicken tenders.
7. Serve straight away.

Nutrition Value:

- Calories: 350
- Fat: 19
- Carbs: 3
- Protein: 23
- Fiber: 2 g

Honey Garlic Chicken and Vegetables

Preparation time: 10 minutes

Cooking time: 2 minutes

Servings: 2

Ingredients:

- 2 chicken thighs, boneless, skinless, cut into bite-size pieces
- ½ pound potatoes, peeled, cubed
- 6 ounces green beans, frozen
- ½ pound carrots, peeled, sliced into ½ -inch rounds

For the Sauce:

- ½ tablespoon minced garlic
- ½ teaspoon dried basil
- ¼ teaspoon ground black pepper
- ¼ teaspoon dried oregano
- ⅛ teaspoon red pepper
- ¼ cup honey
- ¼ cup of soy sauce
- 2 tablespoons ketchup

Method:

1. Take a small bowl, place all the ingredients for the sauce, and then whisk until combined.
2. Turn on the Instant Pot Duo Crisp Air Fryer, pour the sauce into the inner pot, add remaining ingredients and then toss until coated.
3. Shut the instant pot with the pressure cooker lid, select the "pressure cook" option, select the high-pressure setting
4. press +/- buttons to adjust the cooking time to 2 minutes and press the start button.
5. When done, do the natural pressure release and then serve.

Nutrition Value:

- Calories: 270
- Fat: 4.4
- Carbs: 35.6
- Protein: 22.8
- Fiber: 4.5 g

Chapter 5: Beef and Pork

Pork Chops

Preparation time: 10 minutes
Cooking time: 30 minutes
Servings: 2

Ingredients:

- ½ cup almond flour
- 4 pork chops
- 1 egg
- ½ cup grated parmesan cheese

Method:

1. Turn on the Instant Pot Duo Crisp Air Fryer, insert the air fryer basket in it, and then grease with oil.
2. Take a shallow dish, crack the egg in it and then whisk until blended.
3. Take a separate shallow dish, add almond flour and cheese and then stir until combined.
4. Working on one pork chop at a time, dip into the egg
5. and then coat in almond-parmesan mixture until dredge.
6. Repeat with the remaining pork chops, arrange them in the air fryer basket in a single layer, spray with oil, and then shut the instant pot with the air fryer lid.
7. Select the "air fryer" option, press +/- buttons to adjust the cooking temperature to 360 degrees F and cooking time to 28 minutes, and then press the start button.
8. Turn the pork chops halfway through and when done, transfer pork chops to a plate and let them rest for 15 minutes.
9. Serve straight away.

Nutrition Value:

- Calories: 502
- Fat: 31
- Carbs: 7
- Protein: 49
- Fiber: 2 g

Pot Roast

Preparation time: 10 minutes
Cooking time: 1 hour and 15 minutes
Servings: 2

Ingredients:

- ½ pound baby potatoes
- 1 pound chuck roast
- 1/3 pound baby carrots
- ½ teaspoon garlic powder
- 1 teaspoon salt
- 2 sprigs of rosemary
- ½ teaspoon ground black pepper
- 1 cup of water

Method:

1. Turn on the Instant Pot Duo Crisp Air Fryer, pour the water into the inner pot, insert a steamer rack, and then place the roast on it.
2. Shut the instant pot with the pressure cooker lid, select the "pressure cook" option, select the high-pressure setting
3. press +/- buttons to adjust the cooking time to 1 hour and press the start button.
4. When done, do the quick pressure release, add carrot and potatoes into the instant pot and then shut with the pressure cooker lid.
5. Select the "pressure cook" option, select the high-pressure setting
6. press +/- buttons to adjust the cooking time to 7 minutes and press the start button.
7. When done, do a natural pressure release for 5 minutes, then do a quick pressure release and then remove the pressure cooker lid.
8. Shut the instant pot with the air fryer lid, select the "air fryer" option, press +/- buttons to adjust the cooking temperature to 450 degrees F, press +/- buttons to adjust the cooking time to 5 minutes, and then press the start button.
9. When done, the top of chicken and vegetables should turn brown and then serve.

Nutrition Value:

- Calories: 456
- Fat: 22

- Carbs: 27
- Protein: 39
- Fiber: 5 g

Sous Vide Steak

Preparation time: 10 minutes
Cooking time: 4 hours and 10 minutes
Servings: 2

Ingredients:

- 2 boneless steaks, about 1 ½ inch thick
- 2 teaspoons salt
- 2 teaspoons ground black pepper
- 2 tablespoons butter, unsalted
- 10 cups water

Method:

1. Turn on the Instant Pot Duo Crisp Air Fryer, fill the inner pot with water until two-third full, and then shut the instant pot with the pressure cooker lid.
2. Select the "sous vide" option, press +/- buttons to adjust the cooking temperature to 137 degrees F and cooking time to 1 hour, and then press the start button.
3. Meanwhile, season the steaks with salt and black pepper until coated, place them into a large plastic ba
4. squeeze out air as much as possible and then seal the bag
5. When the water into the instant pot reaches its set temperature, lower the steak bag in it and then shut the instant pot with the pressure cooker lid.
6. Select the "sous vide" option, press +/- buttons to adjust the cooking temperature to 156 degrees F and cooking time to 3 hours, and then press the start button.
7. The steaks should be well done, and when done, remove the steak bag from the instant pot, take out the steaks and then pat dry.
8. Drain the inner pot, press the sauté button, add butter and then let it melt.
9. Add a steak, sear it for 1 to 2
10. per side until golden brown and then transfer to a plate.
11. Repeat with the remaining steaks and then serve.

Nutrition Value:

- Calories: 402
- Fat: 26
- Carbs: 1
- Protein: 38
- Fiber: 0 g

Beef Brisket

Preparation time: 10 minutes
Cooking time: 55 minutes
Servings: 2

Ingredients:

- 1 pound beef brisket
- 1 ½ teaspoon salt
- ½ teaspoon ground black pepper
- 1/3 tablespoon paprika
- 1 cup of water

For the Sauce:

- 1/3 tablespoon minced garlic
- ¼ teaspoon salt
- 1/3 tablespoon paprika
- 2/3 tablespoon barbecue seasoning
- ¼ teaspoon ground black pepper
- 1/3 teaspoon cayenne pepper
- 1/3 teaspoon cornflour

Method:

1. Prepare the beef and for this, score it with a sharp knife and then rub with salt, black pepper, and paprika.
2. Turn on the Instant Pot Duo Crisp Air Fryer, pour the water into the inner pot, insert a steamer basket in it, and then arrange the prepared beef on top.
3. Shut the instant pot with the pressure cooker lid, select the "pressure cook" option, select the high-pressure setting
4. press +/- buttons to adjust the cooking time to 40 minutes and press the start button.
5. When the instant pot beef, do a quick pressure release, open the instant pot, transfer the beef brisket to a cutting board and then season with some more salt, black pepper, and paprika.

6. Reserve the stock from the inner pot, insert the air fryer basket in it, grease it with oil and then place the beef brisket in it.

7. Shut the instant pot with the air fryer lid, select the "air fryer" option, press +/- buttons to adjust the cooking temperature to 360 degrees F, and cook for 5

8. until beef turns crisp.

9. When done, transfer brisket to a plate and let it rest until required.

10. Then, prepare the sauce and for this, remove the air fryer basket and then pour 1 cup of reserved stock into the inner pot.

11. Add all the ingredients for the sauce in it, whisk until combined, and then cook for 3 to 5

12. until sauce has thickened.

13. Cut the beef brisket into slices, drizzle with sauce and then serve.

Nutrition Value:

- Calories: 246
- Fat: 16
- Carbs: 0
- Protein: 24
- Fiber: 0 g

Meatloaf

Preparation time: 10 minutes
Cooking time: 20 minutes
Servings: 2

Ingredients:

- 1 teaspoon olive oil
- ¼ of a small white onion, peeled, chopped
- ½ pound ground beef
- 2 tablespoons breadcrumbs
- 1 tablespoon ketchup
- ½ teaspoon Worcestershire sauce
- ½ teaspoon Italian seasoning
- ¼ teaspoon garlic powder
- ¼ teaspoon salt
- 1/8 teaspoon ground black pepper
- ½ of egg
- 1 tablespoon ketchup
- ½ tablespoon mustard paste

Method:

1. Take a medium skillet pan, place it over medium heat, add oil and then let it heat.
2. Meanwhile, add onion, cook for 5
3. or until sauté and then transfer onion to a large bowl.
4. Add remaining ingredients into the onion bowl except for ½ tablespoon ketchup and mustard and then stir until combined.
5. Turn on the Instant Pot Duo Crisp Air Fryer and then insert the air fryer basket.
6. Take a 4-by-6 inch loaf pan, spoon the beef mixture in it and then place the pan into the air fryer basket.
7. Shut the instant pot with the air fryer lid, select the "air fryer" option, press +/- buttons to adjust the cooking temperature to 370 degrees F and cooking time to 10 minutes, and then press the start button.
8. Meanwhile, take a small bowl, place ketchup and mustard in it, and then stir until combined.
9. When the instant pot beeps, spread ketchup mixture over the meatloaf and then continue air frying for 5
10. or more until the top caramelizes.
11. When done, let the meatloaf rest for 10 minutes, cut it into slices, and then serve.

Nutrition Value:

- Calories: 228
- Fat: 7.5
- Carbs: 10.7
- Protein: 27.8
- Fiber: 3.4 g

Pork Carnitas

Preparation time: 10 minutes
Cooking time: 1 hour and 30 minutes
Servings: 2

Ingredients:

- 2 pounds pork shoulder, bone-in
- 1 medium white onion, peeled, chopped
- 1 teaspoon salt
- ¼ teaspoon ground black pepper
- ½ teaspoon red chili powder

- ½ teaspoon orange zest
- ½ teaspoon ground cumin
- ½ teaspoon dried oregano
- 1 tablespoon olive oil

Method:

1. Prepare the pork and for this, mix together salt, black pepper, chili powder, orange zest, cumin, and oregano and then rub this mixture on all sides of the pork shoulder until coated.
2. Turn on the Instant Pot Duo Crisp Air Fryer, add oil into the inner pot and when hot, add onion and then cook for 5
3. until tender.
4. Add prepared pork, shut the instant pot with the pressure cooker lid, select the "pressure cook" option, select the high-pressure settin
5. press +/- buttons to adjust the cooking time to 1 hour and 15 minutes, and then press the start button.
6. When the instant pot beeps, do the natural pressure release, transfer pork to a cutting board, and then reserve the cooking liquid and onion in a bowl.
7. Let the pork rest for 10 minutes, shred it with two forks, and then add to the instant pot.
8. Shut the instant pot with the air fryer lid, set the cooking temperature to 400 degrees F, and then cook for 12 minutes.
9. When done, the pork should be crisp, then uncover the instant pot, toss the pork with tongs and if it is not crisp, continue air frying for another 3 minutes.
10. When done, pour ½ cup of the reserved cooking liquid into the pork, stir until well combined, and then serve.

Nutrition Value:

- Calories: 532.7
- Fat: 37.3
- Carbs: 0
- Protein: 53.3
- Fiber: 0 g

Pork Tenderloin

Preparation time: 10 minutes

Cooking time: 20 minutes

Servings: 2

Ingredients:

- ¾ pound pork tenderloin
- ¼ teaspoon onion powder
- 1/8 teaspoon garlic powder
- ¾ teaspoon salt
- ¼ teaspoon ground black pepper
- ½ tablespoon paprika
- 1 tablespoon brown sugar
- ½ teaspoon mustard powder
- 1/8 teaspoon cayenne pepper
- ½ tablespoon olive oil

Method:

1. Place all the spices in a small bowl, and then stir until mixed.
2. Rub the pork with oil, and then rub with the spice mix until coated.
3. Turn on the Instant Pot Duo Crisp Air Fryer, insert the air fryer basket, and grease with oil.
4. Place the prepared pork tenderloin in it, shut the instant pot with the air fryer lid, select the "air fryer" option, press +/- buttons to adjust the cooking temperature to 400 degrees F, and cooking time to 20 minutes, and then press the start button.
5. When done, transfer the pork tenderloin to a cutting board, let it rest for 5 minutes, and then cut it into slices.
6. Serve straight away.

Nutrition Value:

- Calories: 333.3
- Fat: 9.1
- Carbs: 0
- Protein: 58.7
- Fiber: 0 g

Beef Stew

Preparation time: 10 minutes

Cooking time: 55 minutes

Servings: 2

Ingredients:

- ¾ pound meat of beef stew
- ½ pound potatoes, peeled, cubed
- 8 ounces baby carrots, cut into slices
- ½ of a large white onion, peeled, chopped
- 1 teaspoon minced garlic
- ½ teaspoon salt
- ½ teaspoon ground black pepper
- 1 tablespoons cornstarch
- ½ teaspoon Italian seasoning
- 1 tablespoon Worcestershire sauce
- ½ tablespoon olive oil
- 5 ounces tomato sauce
- 1 tablespoon water
- 1 ½ cups beef broth

Method:

1. Turn on the Instant Pot Duo Crisp Air Fryer, press the sauté button, add oil and then let it heat.
2. Add the beef, season with salt, black pepper, and Italian seasoning
3. and then cook the beef for 3 to 4
4. per side until nicely browned.
5. Pour in the beef broth, stir well, add onion, potatoes, carrots, and garlic, pour in the Worcestershire sauce and tomato sauce, and then stir until mixed.
6. Shut the instant pot with the pressure cooker lid, select the "pressure cook" option, press +/- buttons to adjust the cooking time to 35 minutes, and press the start button.
7. When done, let the pressure release naturally, open the instant pot, and then stir the stew.
8. Stir together cornstarch and water, add to the stew, and then stir until well mixed.
9. Press the sauté button, cook the stew for 3 to 5
10. until thickened, and then serve.

Nutrition Value:

- Calories: 384
- Fat: 12
- Carbs: 23
- Protein: 42
- Fiber: 3 g

Burnt Ends

Preparation time: 10 minutes
Cooking time: 15 minutes
Servings: 2

Ingredients:

- 2/3 pound chuck roast, scored
- ½ teaspoon minced garlic
- ½ teaspoon garlic powder
- ¼ tablespoon salt
- ¼ tablespoon ground black pepper
- ¼ teaspoon liquid smoke
- 1 teaspoon brown sugar
- 1 ½ tablespoon apple cider vinegar
- ½ tablespoon honey
- 1/3 cup barbecue sauce

Method:

1. Cut the meat into 1-inch pieces, place them in a large bowl and then rub with garlic powder, salt, and black pepper until well coated.
2. Turn on the Instant Pot Duo Crisp Air Fryer, add minced garlic, pour in the vinegar and liquid smoke, and whisk until combined.
3. Add seasoned roast pieces into the instant pot, shut the instant pot with the pressure cooker lid, select the "pressure cook" option, press +/- buttons to adjust the cooking time to 4 minutes, and press the start button.
4. Meanwhile, pour the barbecue sauce into a bowl, add sugar and honey and then whisk until combined.
5. When done, do a natural pressure release, transfer meat pieces to a large bowl, add prepared sauce and then toss until coated.
6. Wipe clean the inner pot, insert the fryer basket in it, arrange prepared roast pieces in a single layer, and then spray with oil.
7. Shut the instant pot with the air fryer lid, select the "air fryer" option, set the cooking temperature to 450 degrees F, and then cook for 8 minutes, turning the roast pieces halfway.
8. Serve straight away.

Nutrition Value:

- Calories: 359
- Fat: 16
- Carbs: 27
- Protein: 27
- Fiber: 1 g

BBQ Baby Back Ribs

Preparation time: 10 minutes

Cooking time: 45 minutes

Servings: 2

Ingredients:

- 1 pound baby back ribs
- 2 tablespoons spicy dry rub
- 3 tablespoons BBQ sauce
- 1/3 cup chicken broth

Method:

1. Turn on the Instant Pot Duo Crisp Air Fryer, pour the chicken broth into the inner pot, and then insert the steamer rack.
2. Sprinkle the spicy dry rub on all sides of baby back ribs, place them into the air fryer basket and then shut with the pressure cooker lid.
3. Select the "pressure cook" option, select the high-pressure setting
4. press +/- buttons to adjust the cooking time to 25 minutes and press the start button.
5. When the instant pot beeps, do natural pressure release, transfer ribs to a cutting board, and brush it with the BBQ sauce.
6. Drain the inner pot, insert the air fryer basket in it, grease it with oil, and then place the baby back ribs in it.
7. Shut the instant pot with the air fryer lid, select the "air fryer" option, select the cooking temperature to 400 degrees F and then cook for 20
8. until crisp, turning halfway.
9. Serve straight away.

Nutrition Value:

- Calories: 389
- Fat: 27

- Carbs: 3
- Protein: 31
- Fiber: 0 g

Country Style Ribs

Preparation time: 40 minutes
Cooking time: 30 minutes
Servings: 2

Ingredients:

- 1 pound country-style ribs
- ¼ teaspoon onion powder
- ¼ teaspoon garlic powder
- ¼ teaspoon salt
- ¼ teaspoon ground black pepper
- ½ tablespoon honey
- ½ tablespoon soy sauce
- ¼ cup apple cider vinegar
- 1/3 cup cold water
- ¼ cup BBQ sauce

Method:

1. Pour water and vinegar into a large plastic ba
2. add garlic powder, onion powder, and soy sauce, seal the bag and shake it well.
3. Add country ribs into the plastic ba
4. add salt, black pepper, and honey, seal the ba
5. turn it upside down until well coated, and then marinate the ribs for 30
6. in the refrigerator.
7. Turn on the Instant Pot Duo Crisp Air Fryer, transfer the ribs mixture into the inner pot, and then shut the instant pot with the pressure cooker lid.
8. Select the "pressure cook" option, select the high-pressure setting
9. press +/- buttons to adjust the cooking time to 15 minutes and press the start button.
10. When done, do a natural pressure release, open the instant pot, transfer the ribs to a plate and then brush with the BBQ sauce.
11. Insert the air fryer basket into the instant pot, grease it with oil, arrange the ribs into the basket and then shut with the air fryer lid.

12. Select the "air fryer" option, set the cooking temperature to 400 degrees F, and then cook for 12

13. until done, turning the ribs halfway.

14. Serve straight away.

Nutrition Value:

- Calories: 373
- Fat: 20
- Carbs: 11
- Protein: 34
- Fiber: 1 g

Spare Ribs

Preparation time: 10 minutes

Cooking time: 30 minutes

Servings: 2

Ingredients:

- 1 rack of spareribs
- 1 teaspoon onion powder
- 1 teaspoon garlic powder
- 1 teaspoon salt
- 1 teaspoon ground black pepper
- 2 tablespoons apple cider vinegar
- 1 cup of water
- ½ cup BBQ sauce

Method:

1. Take a small bowl, place onion powder and garlic powder in it, add vinegar and then stir until mixed.

2. Brush the vinegar mixture all over the ribs, season with salt and black pepper, and then let it marinate for 30

3. in the refrigerator.

4. Turn on the Instant Pot Duo Crisp Air Fryer, pour the water into the inner pot, insert the steamer rack, and then arrange the ribs on it.

5. Shut the instant pot with the pressure cooker lid, select the "pressure cook" option, press +/- buttons to adjust the cooking time to 25 minutes, and press the start button.

6. When done, do a natural pressure release, open the instant pot, transfer the ribs to a plate and then brush with the BBQ sauce.

7. Insert the air fryer basket into the instant pot, grease it with oil, arrange the ribs into the basket and then shut with the air fryer lid.

8. Select the "air fryer" option, set the cooking temperature to 400 degrees F, and then cook for 12

9. until done, turning the ribs halfway.

10. Serve straight away.

Nutrition Value:

- Calories: 396
- Fat: 31
- Carbs: 8

- Protein: 20
- Fiber: 1 g

Pulled Pork

Preparation time: 10 minutes
Cooking time: 1 hour and 35 minutes
Servings: 2

Ingredients:

- 1 pound pork roast, boneless
- 1/3 teaspoon garlic powder
- 2/3 teaspoon salt
- 1/3 teaspoon ground black pepper

- 1/8 teaspoon red pepper flakes
- ¼ cup BBQ sauce
- 1/3 cup chicken broth

Method:

1. Turn on the Instant Pot Duo Crisp Air Fryer, place roast into the inner pot, add garlic powder, salt, black pepper, and red pepper flakes, and then pour in the broth.

2. Shut the instant pot with the pressure cooker lid, select the "pressure cook" option, press +/- buttons to adjust the cooking time to 1 hour and 30 minutes, and then press the start button.

3. When done, do a natural pressure release, open the instant pot, transfer it to the cutting board and then shred the roast with two forks.

4. Press the sauté button, bring the cooking liquid in the inner pot to boil, whisk in BBQ sauce and then continue cooking it for 5

5. until the sauce has reduced by half.

6. Add the shredded beef, toss until coated, and then cook for 2 minutes.

7. Serve straight away.

Nutrition Value:

- Calories: 268
- Fat: 7
- Carbs: 2

- Protein: 43
- Fiber: 0 g

Honey Garlic Ribs

Preparation time: 10 minutes

Cooking time: 35 minutes

Servings: 2

Ingredients:

- 1 pound baby back ribs
- 2 teaspoons minced garlic
- ¼ teaspoon ground black pepper
- 2 tablespoons honey

- 1 tablespoon olive oil
- 2 tablespoons soy sauce
- 1 cup of water

For the Marinade:

- 1 teaspoon garlic powder
- ¼ teaspoon salt
- 1 tablespoon soy sauce

- ¼ teaspoon sesame oil
- 1 tablespoon water

Method:

1. Place all the ingredients for the marinade in a large plastic bag, add the ribs, seal the ba

2. turn it upside down until coated, and then let the ribs marinate for a minimum of 30

3. in the refrigerator.

4. Meanwhile, prepare the honey-garlic sauce and for this, turn on the Instant Pot Duo Crisp Air Fryer, press the sauté button and then add oil.

5. Add garlic, cook for 30 seconds, add black pepper, soy sauce, and honey, stir until combined, and then cook the sauce for 1 to 2

6. until thickened slightly.

7. When done, transfer the sauce into a bowl and then set aside until required.

8. Wipe clean the inner pot, pour in the water, insert the steamer rack, and then place the marinated ribs on it.

9. Shut the instant pot with the pressure cooker lid, select the "pressure cook" option, press +/- buttons to adjust the cooking time to 20 minutes, and press the start button.

10. When the instant pot, do a natural pressure release, open the instant pot, transfer the ribs to a plate and then brush with the prepared sauce.

11. Insert the air fryer basket into the instant pot, grease it with oil, arrange the ribs into the basket and then shut with the air fryer lid.

12. Select the "air fryer" option, set the cooking temperature to 400 degrees F, and then cook for 12

13. until done, turning the ribs halfway.

14. Serve straight away.

Nutrition Value:

- Calories: 357
- Fat: 23
- Carbs: 15
- Protein: 23
- Fiber: 1 g

Chapter 6: Seafood and Fish

Salmon with Dill Sauce

Preparation time: 5 minutes
Cooking time: 8 minutes
Servings: 2

Ingredients:

- 2 fillets of salmon, each about 1 ½ inch thick
- ¾ teaspoon salt
- ½ teaspoon ground black pepper
- ½ teaspoon paprika
- 1 tablespoon olive oil

For the Sauce:

- 4 tablespoons sour cream
- 4 tablespoons mayonnaise
- ½ teaspoon minced garlic
- 1 tablespoon lemon juice
- ¼ teaspoon mustard paste
- 1 teaspoon dried dill

Method:

1. Turn on the Instant Pot Duo Crisp Air Fryer, insert the fryer basket, and then grease it with oil.
2. Meanwhile, prepare the salmon and for this, brush it with oil and then season with salt, black pepper, and paprika.
3. Arrange the prepared fillets on the fryer basket and then shut the instant pot with the air fryer lid.
4. Select the "air fryer" option, press +/- buttons to adjust the cooking temperature to 390 degrees F and cooking time to 8 minutes, and then press the start button.
5. Cook the salmon until tender and golden brown, turning it halfway.
6. While salmon cooks, prepare the sauce, and for this, take a small bowl, place all of its ingredients in it and then whisk until combined.
7. Serve the salmon with the prepared sauce.

Nutrition Value:

- Calories: 702
- Fat: 53

- Carbs: 2
- Protein: 51
- Fiber: 0 g

Tuna Steaks

Preparation time: 5 minutes
Cooking time: 8 minutes
Servings: 2

Ingredients:

- 2 tuna steaks, each about 6 ounces
- 2 teaspoons bagel spice blend
- 1 tablespoon olive oil

Method:

1. Turn on the Instant Pot Duo Crisp Air Fryer, insert the fryer basket, and then grease it with oil.
2. Meanwhile, prepare the tuna and for this, brush the steaks with oil and then season with the spice blend.
3. Arrange the prepared tuna steaks on the fryer basket and then shut the instant pot with the air fryer lid.
4. Select the "air fryer" option, press +/- buttons to adjust the cooking temperature to 390 degrees F and cooking time to 8 minutes, and then press the start button.
5. When done, transfer the steaks to a plate, let them rest for 5 minutes, and then serve.

Nutrition Value:

- Calories: 125
- Fat: 4
- Carbs: 0
- Protein: 21
- Fiber: 0 g

Lemon Pepper Salmon

Preparation time: 10 minutes
Cooking time: 5 minutes

Servings: 2

Ingredients:

- 2/3 pound salmon, skin-on
- 2/3 of a medium zucchini, cut into juliennes
- ½ of a lemon, sliced
- 2/3 of medium red bell pepper, cut into juliennes
- 1 sprig of parsley
- 2/3 of a medium carrot, cut into juliennes
- ½ teaspoon salt
- 1 sprig of dill
- 1/3 teaspoon ground black pepper
- 1 sprig of basil
- 2 teaspoons olive oil
- ½ cup of water

Method:

1. Turn on the Instant Pot Duo Crisp Air Fryer, pour water into the inner pot, add parsley, dill and basil and then insert the steamer rack in the inner pot.
2. Brush the salmon with oil, season with salt and black pepper, arrange the salmon on the rack, and then cover with lemon slices.
3. Shut the instant pot with the pressure cooker lid, select the "steam" option, select the high-pressure setting
4. press +/- buttons to adjust the cooking time to 3 minutes and press the start button.
5. When done, do a quick pressure release, carefully open the instant pot and then transfer salmon to a plate.
6. Remove the steamer rack from the inner pot, discard the herb sprigs, add vegetables into the instant pot and then shut with the lid.
7. Press the "sauté" button, press +/- buttons to adjust the cooking time to 2 minutes, and then press the start button.
8. Transfer the vegetables to the salmon plate and then serve.

Nutrition Value:

- Calories: 296
- Fat: 15
- Carbs: 8
- Protein: 31
- Fiber: 2 g

Shrimp Fried Rice

Preparation time: 10 minutes
Cooking time: 22 minutes
Servings: 2

Ingredients:

- ¼ pound shrimps, peeled, deveined
- ½ cup chopped white onion
- ½ of a large carrot, peeled, cut into 1-inch pieces
- ½ cup frozen peas
- 1 teaspoon minced garlic
- ¼ teaspoon salt
- ¼ teaspoon ground black pepper
- 1 ½ tablespoon soy sauce
- ½ cup rice, rinsed
- 2 tablespoons olive oil, divided
- ¼ teaspoon sesame oil
- ½ cup water
- 1 egg

Method:

1. Turn on the Instant Pot Duo Crisp Air Fryer, add ½ tablespoon oil, press the sauté button and then let it heat.
2. Crack the egg in a bowl, whisk until combined, pour into the inner pot and then cook for 2 to 3
3. until scrambled to the desired level.
4. When done, transfer the scrambled eggs to a plate, add peas into the inner pot and then cook for 2 to 3
5. until thoroughly hot and the water evaporates.
6. When done, transfer peas to a separate plate, add 1 tablespoon oil into the inner pot, and let it heat.
7. Add the shrimps into the single layer and then cook for 1 to 2
8. per side until shrimps turn pink.
9. Transfer the shrimps to a plate and then repeat with the remaining shrimps.
10. Add remaining oil into the inner pot, add onion and garlic and then cook for 2
11. until tender.
12. Add rice, stir until cook and then cook for 20 seconds or until sauté.

13. Return the shrimps into the inner pot, add carrot, season with salt and black pepper, pour in the water, and shut the instant pot with the pressure cooker lid.
14. Select the "pressure cook" option, select the high-pressure setting
15. press +/- buttons to adjust the cooking time to 3 minutes and press the start button.
16. When done, do a quick pressure release, open the lid, and then add scrambled eggs and peas.
17. Drizzle with sesame oil and soy sauce, toss until combined, and then let the rice rest for 10 minutes.
18. Serve straight away.

Nutrition Value:

- Calories: 321
- Fat: 11
- Carbs: 41
- Protein: 10
- Fiber: 1 g

Cod with Lemon

Preparation time: 5 minutes
Cooking time: 8 minutes
Servings: 2

Ingredients:

- 2 fillets of cod, each about 4 ounces
- 6 slices of lemon
- ½ teaspoon salt
- 1/3 teaspoon ground black pepper
- 2 teaspoons butter, unsalted
- 1 cup of water

Method:

1. Turn on the Instant Pot Duo Crisp Air Fryer, pour water into the inner pot, and then insert the steamer rack in it.
2. Season the fillets with salt and black pepper, arrange them on the steamer rack, and then cover with lemon slices.

3. Shut the instant pot with the pressure cooker lid, select the "pressure cook" option, select the high-pressure setting

4. press +/- buttons to adjust the cooking time to 8 minutes and press the start button.

5. When done, do a quick pressure release, open the lid, and then serve.

Nutrition Value:

- Calories: 318.7
- Fat: 13
- Carbs: 6.7
- Protein: 41.7
- Fiber: 0.3 g

Butter Shrimps

Preparation time: 5 minutes
Cooking time: 18 minutes
Servings: 2

Ingredients:

- 1 pound large shrimp, peeled, deveined

For the Marinade:

- ½ teaspoon grated ginger
- ½ teaspoon minced garlic
- 1 teaspoon garam masala
- ¾ teaspoon salt
- 1 teaspoon ground cumin
- 1 teaspoon sweet paprika
- 1 teaspoon lime juice
- 2 tablespoons yogurt

For the Sauce:

- 1 shallot, peeled, minced
- 14 ounces diced tomatoes with juice
- ½ teaspoon minced garlic
- ¾ teaspoon grated ginger
- ¼ teaspoon salt
- ¼ teaspoon red pepper flakes
- ¼ teaspoon lime zest
- ½ cup heavy cream
- 2 tablespoons butter, unsalted

For Serving:

- 1 cup cooked rice

Method:

1. Take a medium bowl, place all the ingredients in it, and then whisk until combined.
2. Add the shrimps, toss until coated, and then let them marinate for a minimum of 15
3. in the refrigerator.
4. Meanwhile, prepare the sauce and for this, turn on the Instant Pot Duo Crisp Air Fryer, press the sauté button, add butter into the inner pot and then let it melt.
5. Add shallots, cook for 5 minutes, then add garlic ginger, salt, and red pepper flakes and then cook for 1 minute.
6. Add tomatoes, pour in heavy cream, stir until mixed, and then bring it to a boil.
7. Shut the instant pot with the pressure cooker lid, select the "pressure cook" option, select the high-pressure setting
8. press +/- buttons to adjust the cooking time to 5 minutes and press the start button.
9. When done, do a natural pressure release, switch on the sauté mode and then simmer the sauce for 4
10. until slightly thickened.
11. Return shrimps along with the marinade into the inner pot, add lime zest, and then cook for 2 to 5
12. until shrimps have turn pink.
13. Serve the shrimps over rice.

Nutrition Value:

- Calories: 224
- Fat: 10
- Carbs: 1.3
- Protein: 32
- Fiber: 0.2 g

Ranch Fish

Preparation time: 10 minutes

Cooking time: 10 minutes

Servings: 2

Ingredients:

- 2 fillets of cod
- 2/3 cup breadcrumbs
- ½ teaspoon garlic powder
- 1 ½ tablespoon ranch seasoning
- 1 lemon, cut into wedges
- 1 egg

Method:

1. Take a shallow dish, place the breadcrumbs in it and then stir in garlic powder and ranch seasoning
2. Take a separate shallow dish, crack the egg in it and then whisk until blended.
3. Working on one fillet at a time, dip it into the egg and then dredge with breadcrumbs until coated.
4. Turn on the Instant Pot Duo Crisp Air Fryer, insert the air-fryer basket, and then grease with oil.
5. Arrange the fillets in a single layer in the air fryer, spray with oil, and then shut the instant pot with the air fryer lid.
6. Select the "air fryer" option, press +/- buttons to adjust the cooking temperature to 400 degrees F and cooking time to 10 minutes, and then press the start button.
7. Cook the cod until tender and nicely golden brown and, when done, serve with lemon wedges.

Nutrition Value:

- Calories: 211.7
- Fat: 9
- Carbs: 14
- Protein: 19.1
- Fiber: 1 g

Halibut with Creamy Cheese Sauce

Preparation time: 10 minutes

Cooking time: 10 minutes

Servings: 2

Ingredients:

- 2 halibut fillets, each about 6 ounces
- ½ tablespoon flour
- 1 teaspoon minced garlic
- 1/3 teaspoon salt and more as needed
- ¼ teaspoon ground black pepper and more as needed
- ½ tablespoon butter, unsalted
- 2 tablespoons white wine
- 2 tablespoons half-and-half
- ¼ cup chicken stock
- 2 tablespoons grated parmesan cheese

Method:

1. Turn on the Instant Pot Duo Crisp Air Fryer, insert the air fryer lid, and then grease it with oil.
2. Stir together salt, black pepper, and garlic powder, and then rub this mixture all over the halibut fillets.
3. Arrange the prepared fillets into the air fryer, spray with oil, and then shut the instant pot with the air fryer lid.
4. Select the "air fryer" option, press +/- buttons to adjust the cooking temperature to 400 degrees F and cooking time to 10 minutes, and then press the start button.
5. Cook the halibut until tender, and then turn the fillets halfway through.
6. Meanwhile, prepare the sauce and for this, take a small saucepan, place it over medium heat, add butter and then let it melt.
7. Stir in garlic and flour, whisk until blended and then cook for 2
8. until mixture begins to turn brown.
9. Whisk in chicken stock and white wine, bring it to a boil, turn heat to a low level and then whisk in salt, black pepper, cheese, and half-and-half until combined.
10. Simmer the sauce for 1 to 2
11. until sauce gets slightly thickened, and then remove the pan from heat.
12. Transfer the fillets to the plates, drizzle with the sauce and then serve.

Nutrition Value:

- Calories: 356
- Fat: 0
- Carbs: 2.5
- Protein: 26.1

- Fiber: 0.2 g

Fish Cakes

Preparation time: 10 minutes
Cooking time: 10 minutes
Servings: 2

Ingredients:

- 10 ounces chopped cod
- 2/3 cup panko bread
- 3 tablespoons chopped cilantro
- ½ of lime, cut into wedges
- 1/8 teaspoon salt
- ¼ teaspoon ground black pepper
- 2 tablespoons sweet chili sauce
- 2 tablespoons mayonnaise
- 1 egg

Method:

1. Turn on the Instant Pot Duo Crisp Air Fryer, insert the air fryer lid, and then grease it with oil.
2. Take a large bowl, place fish in it, add cilantro, salt, black pepper, salt, chili sauce, and mayonnaise, stir until well combined, and then shape the mixture into four evenly size patties.
3. Arrange the fish patties into the air fryer, spray with oil, and then shut the instant pot with the air fryer lid.
4. Select the "air fryer" option, press +/- buttons to adjust the cooking temperature to 400 degrees F and cooking time to 10 minutes, and then press the start button.
5. Cook the fish cakes until golden brown, flipping halfway, and then serve.

Nutrition Value:

- Calories: 399
- Fat: 15.5
- Carbs: 27.9
- Protein: 34.6
- Fiber: 2.8 g

Fish Tacos

Preparation time: 10 minutes
Cooking time: 15 minutes
Servings: 2

Ingredients:

For the Fish:

- ¼ pound halibut fillets, cut into 1-inch strips
- 1 tablespoon taco seasoning mix
- ¼ cup breadcrumbs
- 1 egg
- ½ tablespoon water

For the Coleslaw:

- ¾ cup shredded cabbage
- ½ teaspoon minced garlic
- 2 tablespoon sliced red onion
- 1/8 teaspoon salt
- 1 tablespoon sour cream
- ½ teaspoon lime juice
- ½ tablespoon mayonnaise

For Serving:

- 4 taco shells

Method:

1. Prepare the coleslaw and for this, take a medium bowl, place all the ingredients except for cabbage in it and then whisk until combined.
2. Add the cabbage, toss until coated, and then let it rest in the refrigerator until chilled.
3. Turn on the Instant Pot Duo Crisp Air Fryer, insert the air fryer lid, and then grease it with oil.
4. Prepare the fish and for this, take a shallow dish, place the taco seasoning mix in it, take another shallow dish, and spread breadcrumbs on it.
5. Take another shallow dish in it, crack the egg in it, add water and then whisk until blended.
6. Working on one fillet at a time, coat it in taco seasoning

7. dip into the egg

8. and then dredge in bread crumb mixture until evenly coated.

9. Arrange the prepared fillets in the air fryer basket, spray with oil, and then shut the instant pot with the air fryer lid.

10. Select the "air fryer" option, press +/- buttons to adjust the cooking temperature to 350 degrees F and cooking time to 14 minutes, and then press the start button.

11. Cook the fillets until thoroughly cooked and crisp, turning the fillets halfway and when done, transfer the fillets to a cutting board.

12. Cut the fillets into bite-size pieces, divide evenly into the taco shells, top with coleslaw and then serve.

Nutrition Value:

- Calories: 250
- Fat: 11
- Carbs: 26
- Protein: 11
- Fiber: 3 g

Chapter 7: Vegetarian and Vegan

Savory Potato Bake

Preparation time: 10 minutes
Cooking time: 23 minutes
Servings: 2

Ingredients:

- 1 cup ham cubes
- 2 ½ cup diced potatoes
- ¼ of a small white onion, peeled, chopped
- 2 teaspoons flour
- ½ teaspoon mustard powder
- 6 tablespoons water
- 2 tablespoons butter, unsalted
- 1 ¼ cup shredded cheddar cheese
- 2/3 cup milk

Method:

1. Turn on the Instant Pot Duo Crisp Air Fryer, pour water into the inner pot, and then add onion and potatoes.
2. Shut the instant pot with the pressure cooker lid, select the "pressure cook" option, select the high-pressure setting
3. press +/- buttons to adjust the cooking time to 8 minutes and press the start button.
4. Meanwhile, take a small saucepan, place it over low heat, add butter and then let it melt.
5. Whisk in mustard and flour until smooth, slowly whisk in milk or until thicken and then whisk in cheese until melted, set aside until required.
6. When done, do a quick pressure release, open the instant pot, add the ham, pour in the cheese sauce and then stir until well combined.
7. Shut the instant pot with the air fryer lid, select the "air fryer" option, press +/- buttons to adjust the cooking temperature to 325 degrees F and cooking time to 15 minutes, and then press the start button.
8. Serve straight away.

- Protein: 12
- Fiber: 7 g

Preparation time: 10 minutes

Cooking time: 28 minutes

Servings: 2

Ingredients:

- 2 potatoes, each about 6 ounces
- 1 teaspoon salt
- ½ teaspoon ground black pepper
- 1 tablespoon chives
- 2 tablespoons butter, unsalted

- 2 tablespoons olive oil
- 2 tablespoons sour cream
- 2 tablespoons grated cheddar cheese1
- 1 cup of water

Method:

1. Turn on the Instant Pot Duo Crisp Air Fryer, pour the water into the inner pot, and then insert the steamer rack in it.
2. Pierce each of the potato with a fork, arrange then on the trivet stand, and then shut the instant pot with the pressure cooker lid.
3. Select the "pressure cooker" option, select the high-pressure settin
4. press +/- buttons to adjust the cooking time to 20 minutes and press the start button.
5. When done, do a natural pressure release, open the instant pot, and then transfer the potatoes to a plate.
6. Drain the inner pot and then insert the air fryer basket in it.
7. Brush the potatoes with oil, season with salt and black pepper, arrange in the air fryer basket and then shut with the air fryer lid.
8. Select the "air fryer" option, press +/- buttons to adjust the cooking temperature to 400 degrees F and cooking time to 8 minutes, and then press the start button.

9. When done, transfer the potatoes to a plate, slice each potato lengthwise and then top with butter, sour cream, and cheese.
10. Serve straight away.

Nutrition Value:

- Calories: 188
- Fat: 2
- Carbs: 37
- Protein: 5
- Fiber: 4 g

Spicy Potato Halves

Preparation time: 10 minutes
Cooking time: 20 minutes
Servings: 2

Ingredients:

- 1/3 pound baby potatoes
- ¼ teaspoon salt
- 1 tablespoon olive oil
- 1 cup of water

For the Spice Mix:

- ¼ teaspoon salt
- ½ teaspoon ground coriander
- 1/3 teaspoon ground cumin
- 1/8 teaspoon ground turmeric
- ¼ teaspoon paprika
- 1/8 teaspoon cayenne pepper

For Garnish:

- ½ tablespoon chopped cilantro
- ½ teaspoon lemon juice

Method:

1. Wash and pat dry the baby potatoes, cut each in half, and then place them in a large bowl.
2. Drizzle oil over the potatoes, season with salt, and then toss until coated.
3. Turn on the Instant Pot Duo Crisp Air Fryer, insert the air fryer basket, and then arrange potatoes in it cut side down.

4. Shut the instant pot with the air fryer lid, select the "air fryer" option, press +/- buttons to adjust the cooking temperature to 400 degrees F and cooking time to 10 minutes, and then press the start button.
5. When done, transfer potatoes to a large bowl, add all the spices, and then toss until well coated.
6. Arrange the seasoned potatoes in the air fryer basket and shut the instant pot with the air fryer lid.
7. Select the "air fryer" option, press +/- buttons to adjust the cooking temperature to 400 degrees F and cooking time to 10 minutes, and then press the start button.
8. Shake the potatoes halfway through, cook the potatoes until crisp, and, when done, transfer potatoes to a plate.
9. Drizzle lemon juice over the potatoes, sprinkle with cilantro, cool the potatoes for 5 minutes, and then serve.

Nutrition Value:

- Calories: 95
- Fat: 5
- Carbs: 11
- Protein: 1
- Fiber: 1 g

Crispy Tofu

Preparation time: 20 minutes
Cooking time: 10 minutes
Servings: 2

Ingredients:

- 8 ounces tofu, extra-firm, pressed, drained
- ½ teaspoon minced garlic
- 1 tablespoon soy sauce
- ½ tablespoon olive oil
- ½ tablespoon sesame oil

Method:

1. Take a small bowl, add garlic to it, pour in soy sauce, olive oil, and sesame oil, and then stir until combined.

2. Cut the tofu into bite-size cubes, arrange them in a baking dish, drizzle with soy sauce mixture, toss until coated, and then let them marinate for 15 minutes.

3. Turn on the Instant Pot Duo Crisp Air Fryer, insert the air fryer basket, and then grease it with oil.

4. Arrange the tofu pieces in a single layer into the air fryer basket and then shut the instant pot with the air fryer lid.

5. Select the "air fryer" option, press +/- buttons to adjust the cooking temperature to 375 degrees F and cooking time to 10 minutes, and then press the start button.

6. Shake the tofu halfway through, cook the tofu until crisp, and, when done, transfer tofu to a plate.

7. Serve straight away.

Nutrition Value:

- Calories: 165
- Fat: 13.2
- Carbs: 3.3

- Protein: 11.1
- Fiber: 0.5 g

Cauliflower Wings

Preparation time: 10 minutes
Cooking time: 15 minutes
Servings: 2

Ingredients:

- 1/3 large head of cauliflower, cut into florets
- ¼ cup all-purpose flour
- 1/3 teaspoon onion powder
- 2/3 teaspoon garlic powder
- 1/8 teaspoon salt
- 1/8 teaspoon ground black pepper

- 1/3 teaspoon paprika
- 1/3 cup red hot sauce
- 1 ½ tablespoon molasses
- 3 tablespoons milk
- 3 tablespoons water
- 2/3 tablespoon butter, unsalted

Method:

1. Turn on the Instant Pot Duo Crisp Air Fryer, insert the air fryer basket, and then grease it with oil.
2. Place flour in a shallow dish, add onion powder, garlic powder, salt, black pepper, and paprika, stir until mixed, and then whisk in milk and water until smooth batter comes together.
3. Working on one floret at a time, dip into the prepared batter, place in the air fryer basket, repeat with the remaining florets and then spray with oil.
4. Shut the instant pot with the air fryer lid, select the "air fryer" option, press +/- buttons to adjust the cooking temperature to 350 degrees F and cooking time to 15 minutes, and then press the start button.
5. Cook the florets until golden brown and crisp, turning halfway, and then transfer florets to a bowl.
6. While florets cook, prepare the sauce and for this, take a small saucepan, place butter in it and then let it melt.
7. Whisk in hot sauce and molasses until well combined, and then remove the pan from heat.
8. When all the florets are fried, transfer them to a bowl, drizzle with prepared sauce and then toss until coated.
9. Serve straight away.

Nutrition Value:

- Calories: 241
- Fat: 7
- Carbs: 40
- Protein: 4
- Fiber: 2 g

Loaded Potato Soup

Preparation time: 10 minutes
Cooking time: 18 minutes
Servings: 2

Ingredients:

- 1/3 of a medium white onion, peeled, diced
- 3 medium potatoes, peeled, 1-inch chopped
- 1/3 tablespoon flour
- ¼ teaspoon minced garlic
- ½ teaspoon salt
- ¼ teaspoon ground black pepper
- 1/3 tablespoon butter, unsalted
- 2/3 cup shredded cheddar cheese
- 1/3 cup milk
- 1 cup chicken broth
- ½ cup cream of chicken soup

Method:

1. Turn on the Instant Pot Duo Crisp Air Fryer, press the sauté button, add butter and then let it melt.
2. Add onion, cook for 2
3. until onion turns soft, stir in garlic and then cook for 1 minute until fragrant.
4. Add potatoes, season with salt and black pepper, pour in the soup and broth and then stir until mixed.
5. Shut the instant pot with the pressure cooker lid, select the "pressure cook" option, select the high-pressure setting
6. press +/- buttons to adjust the cooking time to 10 minutes and press the start button.
7. Meanwhile, place flour in a small bowl and then whisk in milk until smooth, set aside until combined.
8. When done, do a quick pressure release, open the instant pot and then stir in flour mixture until incorporated.
9. Press the sauté button, cook the soup for 5
10. until thickened, and then stir in cheese until melted.
11. Serve straight away.

Nutrition Value:

- Calories: 481
- Fat: 26
- Carbs: 43
- Protein: 19
- Fiber: 2 g

Pizza Pasta

Preparation time: 5 minutes
Cooking time: 18 minutes
Servings: 2

Ingredients:

- 12 ounces diced tomatoes with juice
- 3 ounces pepperoni, sliced
- ½ of a medium white onion, peeled, chopped
- 1 teaspoon minced garlic
- ¼ teaspoon dried oregano
- ¼ teaspoon salt
- ¼ teaspoon dried basil
- ¼ teaspoon ground black pepper
- ¼ teaspoon red pepper flakes
- 12 ounces tomato puree
- 1 cup vegetable stock
- 1 cup pasta
- 4 ounces shredded mozzarella cheese

Method:

1. Turn on the Instant Pot Duo Crisp Air Fryer, press the sauce button, and let it heat.
2. Add onion, and garlic, cook for 5
3. until nicely browned, then stir in all the spices and cook for 1 minute.
4. Pour in the stock, stir until mixed, and then stir in tomatoes and tomato puree until combined.
5. Top the mixture with pasta, press it gently until immersed but don't stir, and then shut the instant pot with the pressure cooker lid.
6. Select the "pressure cook" option, select the high-pressure setting
7. press +/- buttons to adjust the cooking time to 6 minutes and press the start button.
8. When done, do a quick pressure release, stir in half of the cheese, sprinkle the remaining cheese on top of pasta, and then shut the instant pot with the air fryer lid.
9. Select the "air fryer" option, press +/- buttons to adjust the cooking temperature to 400 degrees F and cooking time to 5 minutes, and then press the start button.

10. Serve straight away.

Nutrition Value:

- Calories: 303
- Fat: 15.5
- Carbs: 21
- Protein: 14
- Fiber: 2 g

Roasted Artichokes

Preparation time: 10 minutes
Cooking time: 25 minutes
Servings: 2

Ingredients:

- 1 large artichoke
- 2 tablespoons minced garlic
- ½ of a lemon, juiced
- 2 tablespoons soy sauce
- 2 tablespoons olive oil
- ½ cup vegetable broth

Method:

1. Prepare the artichokes and for this, cut off its bottom stem, remove the sharp tips, and then pull the leaves.
2. Take a small bowl, place 1 tablespoon garlic, lemon juice, soy sauce, and oil in it, stir until combined, and then brush this mixture all over the artichoke, reserving the marinade for later use.
3. Turn on the Instant Pot Duo Crisp Air Fryer, pour the vegetable broth in it, stir in remaining garlic and then arrange the artichokes in it, stem-side down.
4. Shut the instant pot with the pressure cooker lid, select the "pressure cook" option, select the high-pressure setting
5. press +/- buttons to adjust the cooking time to 20 minutes and press the start button.
6. When done, do a quick pressure release and then transfer artichokes to a cutting board.

7. Let the artichoke rest for 5 minutes, cut each in half, and then drizzle the remaining marinade between the leaves.
8. Drain the inner pot, insert the air fryer basket in it, arrange the artichokes in it cut-side up, and then shut the instant pot with the air fryer lid.
9. Select the "air fryer" option, press +/- buttons to adjust the cooking temperature to 400 degrees F and cooking time to 5 minutes, and then press the start button.
10. Serve straight away.

Nutrition Value:

- Calories: 178
- Fat: 14
- Carbs: 13

- Protein: 4
- Fiber: 4 g

Spaghetti

Servings: 2
Preparation time: 5 minutes
Cooking time: 8 minutes

Ingredients:

- 1 tablespoon garlic powder
- ½ teaspoon salt
- 2 teaspoons Italian herbs
- ¼ teaspoon ground black pepper
- 2 tablespoons nutritional yeast

- 12 ounces marinara sauce
- 8 ounces coconut milk, unsweetened
- 1/3 cup water
- 5 ounces spaghetti

Method:

1. Turn on the Instant Pot Duo Crisp Air Fryer, break spaghetti in half, place it in the inner pot and then add remaining ingredients, don't stir.
2. Shut the instant pot with the pressure cooker lid, select the "pressure cook" option, select the high-pressure setting
3. press +/- buttons to adjust the cooking time to 8 minutes and press the start button.

4. When done, do a quick pressure release, stir the spaghetti and then serve.

Nutrition Value:

- Calories: 438
- Fat: 12
- Carbs: 69.9
- Protein: 12.8
- Fiber: 5.7 g

Zucchini and Tomato Mélange

Preparation time: 5 minutes
Cooking time: 10 minutes
Servings: 2

Ingredients:

- 3 medium zucchinis, chopped
- 1 medium white onion, peeled, sliced
- ½ teaspoon minced garlic
- ½ pound cherry tomatoes
- ½ bunch of basil
- ½ teaspoon salt
- 1 tablespoon olive oil and more as needed
- ½ cup tomato puree

Method:

1. Turn on the Instant Pot Duo Crisp Air Fryer, press the sauté button, add oil and then let it heat.
2. Add onion, cook for 5
3. until soft, then stir in cherry tomato, zucchini and tomato puree and season the mixture with salt.
4. Shut the instant pot with the pressure cooker lid, select the "pressure cook" option, press +/- buttons to adjust the cooking time to 5 minutes, and then press the start button.
5. When done, do a natural pressure release, stir in garlic and then strain the vegetables into a bowl by using a slotted spoon.
6. Sprinkle some more oil over the vegetables, sprinkle with basil leaves and then serve.

Nutrition Value:

- Calories: 83.6
- Fat: 0.5
- Carbs: 19
- Protein: 4
- Fiber: 3.1s g

Chapter 8: Snacks and Appetizers

French Fries

Preparation time: 10 minutes
Cooking time: 20 minutes
Servings: 2

Ingredients:

- 1 large potato
- ½ teaspoon salt
- ½ teaspoon ground black pepper
- ½ teaspoon paprika
- 1 ½ tablespoon olive oil

Method:

1. Turn on the Instant Pot Duo Crisp Air Fryer, insert the air fryer basket, and then grease it with oil.
2. Cut the potatoes into ¼-inch thick fries, place them in a large bowl, add remaining ingredients, and then toss until coated.
3. Add the fries into the air fryer basket, shut with the air fryer lid, select the "air fryer" option, press +/- buttons to adjust the cooking temperature to 375 degrees F and cooking time to 10 minutes, and then press the start button.
4. Shake the fries halfway, continue cooking them for another 10
5. until golden brown and crisp and then serve.

Nutrition Value:

- Calories: 83
- Fat: 3.5
- Carbs: 12
- Protein: 1.5
- Fiber: 1.5 g

Sweet Potato Fries

Preparation time: 5 minutes
Cooking time: 10 minutes

Servings: 2

Ingredients:

- 1 large sweet potato
- 1 tablespoon dried thyme
- 1 tablespoon of sea salt
- 1 tablespoon dried basil
- 2 tablespoons olive oil

Method:

1. Turn on the Instant Pot Duo Crisp Air Fryer, insert the air fryer basket, and then grease it with oil.
2. Cut the potatoes into ¼-inch thick fries, place them in a large bowl, add remaining ingredients, and then toss until coated.
3. Add the fries into the air fryer basket, shut with the air fryer lid, select the "air fryer" option, press +/- buttons to adjust the cooking temperature to 400 degrees F and cooking time to 5 minutes, and then press the start button.
4. Shake the fries halfway, continue cooking them for another 5
5. until golden brown and crisp and then serve.

Nutrition Value:

- Calories: 101
- Fat: 7
- Carbs: 9
- Protein: 1
- Fiber: 2 g

Fried Pickles

Preparation time: 10 minutes
Cooking time: 10 minutes
Servings: 2

Ingredients:

- ¼ cup panko breadcrumbs
- 1 cup dill pickles
- ½ tablespoon garlic powder
- ½ teaspoon Cajun seasoning
- ¼ cup Italian style breadcrumbs
- 2 tablespoons parmesan cheese
- 1 egg

Method:

1. Turn on the Instant Pot Duo Crisp Air Fryer, insert the air fryer basket, and then grease it with oil.
2. Take a shallow dish, place both breadcrumbs in it, add garlic powder, Cajun seasoning
3. and cheese and then stir until combined.
4. Take a separate shallow dish, crack the egg in it and then whisk until blended.
5. Working on one dill pickle at a time, dip into the egg and then coat with breadcrumbs mixture.
6. Arrange the prepared dill pickles in the air fryer basket, spray with oil, and then shut the instant pot with the air fryer lid.
7. Select the "air fryer" option, press +/- buttons to adjust the cooking temperature to 360 degrees F and cooking time to 7 minutes, and then press the start button.
8. Then turn the dill pickles, continue frying them for 3
9. until pickles turn golden brown and crisp, and then serve.

Nutrition Value:

- Calories: 150
- Fat: 5
- Carbs: 17
- Protein: 8
- Fiber: 2 g

Kale Chips

Servings: 2
Preparation time: 5 minutes
Cooking time: 18 minutes

Ingredients:

- ½ pound kale, destemmed, leaves chopped
- 1 teaspoon salt
- 1 tablespoon olive oil

For the Seasoning Mix:

- ¼ teaspoon cayenne pepper
- 1 teaspoon smoked paprika

- 1 teaspoon sesame seeds
- 4 teaspoons nutritional yeast

Method:

1. Turn on the Instant Pot Duo Crisp Air Fryer, insert the air fryer basket, and then grease it with oil.
2. Rinse the chopped kale, drain it well by using a salad spinner and then place kale into a large bowl.
3. Add oil, salt, and all the ingredients for the seasoning mix, toss until coated, and then massage the kale for 1 minute.
4. Spread half of the kale leaves into the air fryer basket and then shut the instant pot with the air fryer lid.
5. Select the "air fryer" option, press +/- buttons to adjust the cooking temperature to 300 degrees F and cooking time to 9 minutes, and then press the start button.
6. Toss the kale chips halfway, then transfer them into a large bowl and repeat with the remaining kale.
7. Serve straight away.

Nutrition Value:

- Calories: 105
- Fat: 8
- Carbs: 7
- Protein: 4
- Fiber: 1 g

Mac and Cheese

Preparation time: 5 minutes
Cooking time: 10 minutes
Servings: 2

Ingredients:

- 1 ¼ cup macaroni
- 1/8 teaspoon garlic powder
- ¼ teaspoon salt
- ¼ teaspoon ground black pepper
- ½ sleeve of ritz cracker
- 4 tablespoons butter, unsalted
- ½ cup heavy cream

- 1 cup and 3 tablespoons shredded cheddar cheese
- 1 cup chicken stock
- 3 tablespoons shredded parmesan cheese

Method:

1. Turn on the Instant Pot Duo Crisp Air Fryer, add 2 tablespoons butter into the inner pot, and then garlic powder and heavy cream.
2. Add macaroni, stir until mixed, and then shut the instant pot with the pressure cooker lid.
3. Select the "pressure cook" option, select the high-pressure setting
4. press +/- buttons to adjust the cooking time to 4 minutes and press the start button.
5. When done, do a quick pressure release, and then stir in 1 cup cheddar cheese and 1 ½ tablespoon parmesan cheese until it melts.
6. Crush the cracker, place it in a small bowl, add remaining butter, stir until combined, and then spoon the mixture over the macaroni.
7. Shut the instant pot with the air fryer lid, select the "air fryer" option, press +/- buttons to adjust the cooking temperature to 400 degrees F and cooking time to 5 minutes, and then press the start button.
8. Serve straight away.

Nutrition Value:

- Calories: 338
- Fat: 28
- Carbs: 11
- Protein: 11
- Fiber: 0.5 g

Tofu Buffalo Bites

Preparation time: 10 minutes
Cooking time: 15 minutes
Servings: 2

Ingredients:

- 12 ounces extra-firm tofu, pressed, drained
- ½ cup chickpea flour
- ¼ cup rice flour
- ½ teaspoon garlic powder
- ½ teaspoon salt
- 1 ½ cup panko breadcrumbs
- ½ cup hot sauce
- 2 tablespoons water

Method:

1. Turn on the Instant Pot Duo Crisp Air Fryer, insert the air fryer basket, and then grease it with oil.
2. Prepare the batter for this, take a shallow dish, place the chickpea flour in it, add salt and garlic powder and then whisk until blended.
3. Take a separate shallow dish and spread rice flour in it, take another shallow dish and then place breadcrumbs in it.
4. Cut the tofu into bite-size pieces, and then working on one tofu piece at a time, coat in rice flour, dip into the chickpea batter and then dredge in breadcrumbs until coated.
5. Arrange the prepared tofu pieces into the air fryer basket, spray with oil, and then shut the instant pot with the air fryer lid.
6. Select the "air fryer" option, press +/- buttons to adjust the cooking temperature to 400 degrees F and cooking time to 7 minutes, and then press the start button.
7. Turn the tofu pieces, continue frying them for another 7 minutes, then transfer the tofu pieces to a plate and then repeat with the remaining tofu pieces.
8. When done, transfer all the tofu pieces to a large bowl, add the buffalo sauce and then toss until coated.
9. Serve straight away.

Nutrition Value:

- Calories: 353
- Fat: 12
- Carbs: 20
- Protein: 21
- Fiber: 7 g

Spinach Artichoke Dip

Preparation time: 10 minutes
Cooking time: 12 minutes
Servings: 2

Ingredients:

- 5 ounces frozen chopped spinach
- 7 ounces artichoke hearts, chopped
- ½ of a medium white onion, peeled, minced
- 1 teaspoon minced garlic
- 1/3 teaspoon salt
- ¼ teaspoon Italian seasoning
- ¼ teaspoon ground black pepper
- 1 ½ tablespoon butter, unsalted
- ¼ cup and 1 tablespoon shredded Gruyere cheese
- 4 ounces cream cheese, softened
- ¼ cup and 1 tablespoon shredded mozzarella cheese
- ¼ cup and 1 tablespoon grated parmesan cheese
- 1 cup water

Method:

1. Turn on the Instant Pot Duo Crisp Air Fryer, press the sauté button, add ¾ tablespoon butter and then let it melt.
2. Add onion and garlic, stir until mixed, and then cook for 3 to 5
3. until onions turn soft.
4. Drain the spinach, squeeze it well to remove excess water, and then place it in a large bowl.
5. Add cream cheese, artichoke hearts, ¼ cup each of all three kinds of cheese and Italian seasoning
6. and then stir until well mixed.
7. Add the onion-butter mixture, season with salt and black pepper, and then stir until combined.
8. Take a cake pan, and then spoon the spinach in it.
9. Wipe clean the inner pot, pour the water in it, insert a steamer rack, and then place the prepared cake pan in it.

10. Shut the instant pot with the pressure cooker lid, select the "pressure cook" option, select the high-pressure setting
11. press +/- buttons to adjust the cooking time to 8 minutes and press the start button.
12. When done, do a natural pressure release, sprinkle remaining cheeses on top, and then shut the instant pot with the air fryer lid.
13. Select the "air fryer" option, press +/- buttons to adjust the cooking temperature to 400 degrees F and cooking time to 4 minutes, and then press the start button.
14. Serve the dip with crackers.

Nutrition Value:

- Calories: 217
- Fat: 18
- Carbs: 6
- Protein: 8
- Fiber: 2 g

Acorn Squash

Preparation time: 10 minutes
Cooking time: 15 minutes
Servings: 2

Ingredients:

- 1 medium acorn squash
- ¼ teaspoon ground black pepper
- 2 tablespoons maple syrup
- 1/8 teaspoon ground nutmeg
- 2 tablespoons melted butter, unsalted
- 1 cup of water

Method:

1. Prepare the squash and for this, cut it in half and then remove its seeds.
2. Turn on the Instant Pot Duo Crisp Air Fryer, pour water into the inner pot, insert a steamer rack and then place the acorn squash halves on it.
3. Shut the instant pot with the pressure cooker lid, select the "pressure cook" option, select the high-pressure setting

4. press +/- buttons to adjust the cooking time to 4 minutes and press the start button.

5. Meanwhile, prepare the butter sauce and for this, take a small bowl and then place the melted butter in it.

6. Add maple syrup and nutme

7. whisk until combined, and then set aside until required.

8. When done, do a natural pressure release, transfer the acorn squash halves to a plate and then apply the butter sauce until coated.

9. Drain the inner pot, place the air fryer basket on it, grease it with oil and then place the prepared acorn squash halves in it.

10. Shut the instant pot with the pressure cooker lid, select the "air fryer" option, press +/- buttons to adjust the cooking temperature to 400 degrees F and cooking time to 10 minutes, and then press the start button.

11. Serve straight away.

Nutrition Value:

- Calories: 121
- Fat: 6
- Carbs: 18
- Protein: 1
- Fiber: 2 g

Honey and Goat Cheese Balls

Preparation time: 25 minutes

Cooking time: 8 minutes

Servings: 2

Ingredients:

- 4 ounces goat cheese, softened
- 3 tablespoons flour
- ¼ cup panko breadcrumbs
- 2 tablespoons honey
- ½ of an egg

Method:

1. Turn on the Instant Pot Duo Crisp Air Fryer, insert the air fryer basket, and then grease it with oil.
2. Divide the cheese into 12 pieces, shape each piece into a ball, arrange the balls on a plate, and then let them freeze for a minimum of 20 minutes.
3. Meanwhile, take a shallow dish and place flour in it, take a separate dish and then place breadcrumbs in it.
4. Take a small bowl, crack the egg in it and then whisk until blended.
5. Working on one cheese ball at a time, coat in flour, dip into the eg
6. and then dredge in breadcrumbs until coated.
7. Arrange the cheese balls into the air fryer basket, spray with oil, and then shut the instant pot with the air fryer lid.
8. Select the "air fryer" option, press +/- buttons to adjust the cooking temperature to 390 degrees F and cooking time to 8 minutes, and then press the start button.
9. Turn the balls halfway through, cook them until nicely golden brown on all sides and then serve.

Nutrition Value:

- Calories: 160.2
- Fat: 10
- Carbs: 6
- Protein: 8
- Fiber: 2 g

Stuffed Mushrooms

Preparation time: 10 minutes
Cooking time: 10 minutes
Servings: 2

Ingredients:

- 8 ounces button mushrooms, destemmed
- ½ teaspoon garlic powder
- ¼ teaspoon salt
- ¼ teaspoon red chili powder
- 1/8 teaspoon ground black pepper
- ¼ teaspoon paprika
- ½ cup grated parmesan cheese
- 4 ounces cream cheese, softened

Method:

1. Remove the stem from the mushrooms, chop them, set aside until required, and then spray the mushroom caps with oil.
2. Place cream cheese in a medium bowl, add salt, black pepper, red chili powder, paprika, and garlic, and then stir until combined.
3. Add the mushroom stems into the cheese mixture, stir until combined, and then stuff this mixture evenly into the mushroom caps.
4. Turn on the Instant Pot Duo Crisp Air Fryer, insert the air fryer basket, and then arrange the stuffed mushrooms in it.
5. Shut the instant pot with the air fryer lid, select the "air fryer" option, press +/- buttons to adjust the cooking temperature to 360 degrees F and cooking time to 8 minutes, and then press the start button.
6. Then top the mushrooms with parmesan cheese and then continue air frying for 1 to 2
7. until cheese melts.
8. Serve straight away.

Nutrition Value:

- Calories: 330
- Fat: 25
- Carbs: 10
- Protein: 15
- Fiber: 5 g

Chapter 9: Desserts

Apple Cobbler

Preparation time: 5 minutes
Cooking time: 15 minutes
Servings: 2

Ingredients:

- 1 can of apple pie fillin
- about 21 ounces
- 7.5 ounces spice cake mix
- ¼ cup melted butter, unsalted
- ¾ cup of water

Method:

1. Turn on the Instant Pot Duo Crisp Air Fryer, pour water into the inner pot, and then insert a steamer rack in it.
2. Take a casserole dish that fits into the Instant Pot Duo Crisp Air Fryer, and then place the apple pie filling in it.
3. Take a medium bowl, place the cake mix in it and then stir in apple until combined.
4. Spoon the prepared cake mix over the apple pie fillin
5. place the casserole dish on top of the steamer rack, and then shut the instant pot with the pressure cooker lid.
6. Select the "pressure cook" option, select the high-pressure setting
7. press +/- buttons to adjust the cooking time to 10 minutes and press the start button.
8. When done, do a natural pressure release, remove the pressure cooker lid, and then shut the instant pot with the air fryer lid.
9. Select the "air fryer" option, press +/- buttons to adjust the cooking temperature to 350 degrees F and cooking time to 5 minutes, and then press the start button.
10. Serve the cobbler with ice cream.

Nutrition Value:

- Calories: 442
- Fat: 14
- Carbs: 80
- Protein: 2
- Fiber: 2 g

Apple Chips

Preparation time: 10 minutes
Cooking time: 20 minutes
Servings: 2

Ingredients:

- 2 medium apples
- 1 teaspoon ground cinnamon

Method:

1. Turn on the Instant Pot Duo Crisp Air Fryer, insert the air fryer basket, and then grease it with oil.
2. Cut the apple into 1/8-inch thick slices using a knife or a mandolin slicer and then remove the seeds.
3. Place the apple slices in a large bowl, sprinkle with cinnamon and then toss until coated.
4. Spread the apple slices in the air fryer basket, spray with oil, and then shut the instant pot with the air fryer lid.
5. Select the "air fryer" option, press +/- buttons to adjust the cooking temperature to 300 degrees F and cooking time to 20 minutes, and then press the start button.
6. Turn the apple chips every 5
7. until the edges begin to curl, and when done, transfer chips to a bowl.
8. Let the chips cool for 5
9. until they turn crispier, and then serve.

Nutrition Value:

- Calories: 97
- Fat: 1
- Carbs: 25
- Protein: 0
- Fiber: 4 g

Peach Cobbler

Preparation time: 10 minutes
Cooking time: 27 minutes
Servings: 2

Ingredients:

For the Filling:

- 2 cups peeled and sliced peaches
- 1/8 teaspoon ground nutmeg
- 1/8 teaspoon salt
- 1/8 teaspoon ground cinnamon
- 2 teaspoons sugar
- 1 cup of water

For the Topping:

- ½ teaspoon baking powder
- 6 tablespoons all-purpose flour
- ¼ teaspoon salt
- 2 tablespoons sugar
- ½ teaspoon powdered sugar
- 2 tablespoons butter, unsalted, softened
- 2 tablespoons milk

Method:

1. Prepare the filling and for this, take a medium bowl, place all of its ingredients in it and then stir until combined.
2. Take two 8-ounce ramekins, and then divide the filling evenly between them.
3. Prepare the topping and for this, take a medium bowl, place flour in it, add salt, sugar, and baking powder, stir until mixed, and then stir in milk until smooth paste forms.
4. Stir in butter until the dough comes together, divide the dough into two pieces and then shape each piece in a round shape.
5. Place a dough piece on top of the filling until fruits have covered and then cover each ramekin tightly with a paper towel and foil.
6. Turn on the Instant Pot Duo Crisp Air Fryer, pour water into the inner pot, insert the steamer rack in it, and then arrange the prepared ramekins on it.

7. Shut the instant pot with the pressure cooker lid, select the "pressure cook" option, select the high-pressure setting

8. press +/- buttons to adjust the cooking time to 20 minutes and press the start button.

9. When done, do a natural pressure release, open the instant pot, remove the cobbler ramekins, uncover them and then sprinkle powdered sugar on top of cobblers.

10. Drain the inner pot, insert the air fryer basket in it, arrange the cobbler ramekin in it and then shut with the air fryer lid.

11. Select the "air fryer" option, press +/- buttons to adjust the cooking temperature to 375 degrees F and cooking time to 7 minutes, and then press the start button.

12. When done, let the cobbler rest for 10

13. and then serve with ice cream.

Nutrition Value:

- Calories: 432
- Fat: 14
- Carbs: 76
- Protein: 4.4
- Fiber: 2.2 g

Brownies

Preparation time: 10 minutes
Cooking time: 15 minutes
Servings: 2

Ingredients:

- ¼ cup all-purpose flour
- 1/8 teaspoon salt
- 3 tablespoons cocoa powder, unsweetened
- 1/8 teaspoon baking powder
- 6 tablespoons sugar
- ¼ teaspoon vanilla extract, unsweetened
- 2 tablespoons butter, unsalted, melted
- 1 egg
- ½ tablespoon olive oil

Method:

1. Turn on the Instant Pot Duo Crisp Air Fryer, and then insert the air fryer basket in it.
2. Take a medium bowl, place flour in it, add remaining ingredients, and then stir until well combined.
3. Take a 7-inch baking pan, grease it with butter and then spoon the batter in it.
4. Place the baking pan into the air fryer, shut the instant pot with the air fryer lid, select the "air fryer" option, press +/- buttons to adjust the cooking temperature to 400 degrees F, and cooking time to 15 minutes, and then press the start button.
5. When done, let the brownies cool for 15
6. in its pan and then cut into squares.
7. Serve straight away.

Nutrition Value:

- Calories: 385
- Fat: 18
- Carbs: 54
- Protein: 6
- Fiber: 3 g

Cherry Cake

Preparation time: 10 minutes
Cooking time: 28 minutes
Servings: 2

Ingredients:

- 20 ounces cherry pie filling
- ½ tablespoon sugar
- ¼ box of yellow cake mix
- 2 tablespoons butter, unsalted, chopped
- 1 cup of water

Method:

1. Take a 7-inch cake pan, grease it with oil and then spoon the cherry pie filling in its bottom.
2. Sprinkle the yellow cake mix over the pie fillin
3. scatter butter on top, and then cover the pan tightly with foil.

4. Turn on the Instant Pot Duo Crisp Air Fryer, pour water into the inner pot, insert the steamer rack, and then place the prepared cake pan on it.

5. Shut the instant pot with the pressure cooker lid, select the "pressure cook" option, select the high-pressure setting

6. press +/- buttons to adjust the cooking time to 25 minutes and press the start button.

7. When done, do a natural pressure release, open the instant pot, take out the baking pan, uncover it and then sprinkle the sugar over the cake.

8. Drain the inner pot, insert the air fryer basket in it, place the cake pan in it, and then shut the instant pot with the air fryer lid.

9. Select the "air fryer" option, press +/- buttons to adjust the cooking temperature to 350 degrees F and cooking time to 3 minutes, and then press the start button.

10. When done, the top of cake should turn golden brown and crisp and then take out the cake pan.

11. Let the cake cool, then cut it into slices, and then serve with ice cream.

Nutrition Value:

- Calories: 259.1
- Fat: 2.4
- Carbs: 56.4
- Protein: 2.9
- Fiber: 1.2 g

Lemon Pudding Cups

Preparation time: 10 minutes
Cooking time: 5 minutes
Servings: 2

Ingredients:

- ½ tablespoon lemon zest
- ½ tablespoon gelatin
- 2 ¼ tablespoon maple syrup
- ½ tablespoon lemon essential oil
- 1 tablespoon lemon juice
- 1 tablespoon coconut oil, melted
- 1 egg
- 1 cup milk
- 1 cup of water

Method:

1. Pour the milk into a blender, add maple syrup, oil, egg
2. lemon juice, lemon zest, and essential oil and then pulse until well combined.
3. Blend in gelatin until just mixed and smooth, divide the pudding evenly among two ½-pint glass jars and then seal with the lid.
4. Turn on the Instant Pot Duo Crisp Air Fryer, pour water into the inner pot, insert the trivet stand, and then place the prepared jars on it.
5. Shut the instant pot with the pressure cooker lid, select the "pressure cook" option, select the high-pressure setting
6. press +/- buttons to adjust the cooking time to 5 minutes and press the start button.
7. When done, do a natural pressure release; take out the glass jars and then let them cool completely.
8. Then transfer the pudding jars into the refrigerator until chilled and then serve.

Nutrition Value:

- Calories: 214
- Fat: 11
- Carbs: 21

- Protein: 7
- Fiber: 1 g

Sweet Apples

Servings: 2
Preparation time: 5 minutes
Cooking time: 8 minutes

Ingredients:

- 3 medium apples, cored, diced
- 2 tablespoons brown sugar
- ¼ teaspoon ground cinnamon
- 1/8 teaspoon ground cloves

- 2 tablespoons white sugar
- 1/8 teaspoon pumpkin pie spice
- 3 tablespoons water

Method:

1. Turn on the Instant Pot Duo Crisp Air Fryer and then insert the air fryer basket.
2. Take a medium heatproof bowl, place apples in it, add remaining ingredients, and then toss until mixed.
3. Place the bowl into the air fryer basket and then shut the air fryer with the air fryer lid.
4. Select the "air fryer" option, press +/- buttons to adjust the cooking temperature to 350 degrees F and cooking time to 6 minutes, and then press the start button.
5. Then stir the apples, continue cooking the apples for 2 minutes, and then serve.

Nutrition Value:

- Calories: 253
- Fat: 1
- Carbs: 66
- Protein: 1
- Fiber: 7 g

Fudgy Chocolate Cake

Preparation time: 10 minutes
Cooking time: 30 minutes
Servings: 2

Ingredients:

- 6 tablespoons flour
- ½ teaspoon baking powder
- ¼ cup of cocoa powder
- ¼ teaspoon salt
- ½ cup of sugar
- ½ teaspoon vanilla extract, unsweetened
- ½ cup of chocolate chips
- ¼ cup butter, unsalted
- 1 egg
- 1 cup of water

Method:

1. Take a large bowl, place butter in it, beat in sugar and vanilla until fluffy, and then beat in egg until well combined.
2. Place flour in a small bowl, add salt, baking powder and cocoa powder and then stir until combined.

3. Stir the flour mixture into the egg mixture until incorporated, and then fold in chocolate chips until just mixed.
4. Take an 8-inch springform pan, grease it with oil, spoon the batter in it, smooth the top, and then cover the pan tightly with foil.
5. Turn on the Instant Pot Duo Crisp Air Fryer, pour the water in it, insert the trivet stand, and then place the springform pan on it.
6. Shut the instant pot with the pressure cooker lid, select the "pressure cook" option, select the high-pressure setting
7. press +/- buttons to adjust the cooking time to 30 minutes, and then press the start button.
8. When done, do a natural pressure release, open the instant pot, and then take out the cake.
9. Let the cake cool for 10 minutes, then cut into slices and serve.

Nutrition Value:

- Calories: 270
- Fat: 11
- Carbs: 40
- Protein: 3
- Fiber: 2 g

Custard

Preparation time: 5 minutes
Cooking time: 7 minutes
Servings: 2

Ingredients:

- 3 tablespoons sugar
- 1/8 teaspoon ground nutmeg
- ½ teaspoon vanilla extract, unsweetened
- 1 cup milk
- 1 ½ egg
- 1 cup of water

Method:

1. Crack the eggs in a medium bowl, add sugar and vanilla, pour in the milk, and then whisk until combined.
2. Pour the batter into a baking dish greased with oil, sprinkle nutmeg on top, and then cover the dish loosely with foil.
3. Turn on the Instant Pot Duo Crisp Air Fryer, pour water into the inner pot, insert the steamer rack and then place the baking dish on it.
4. Shut the instant pot with the pressure cooker lid, select the "pressure cook" option, select the high-pressure setting
5. press +/- buttons to adjust the cooking time to 7 minutes and press the start button.
6. When done, do a quick pressure release, take out the baking dish, and then uncover it.
7. Serve straight away.

Nutrition Value:

- Calories: 186
- Fat: 7
- Carbs: 22
- Protein: 7
- Fiber: 5 g

Rice Pudding

Preparation time: 5 minutes
Cooking time: 5 minutes
Servings: 2

Ingredients:

- ½ cup rice, uncooked
- ¼ cup raisins
- ¼ cup sugar
- ½ teaspoon ground cinnamon
- 1/16 teaspoon salt
- ½ tablespoon butter, unsalted
- 1 cup milk
- ½ cup water

Method:

1. Turn on the Instant Pot Duo Crisp Air Fryer, add rice, add remaining ingredients in it except for butter and then stir until well mixed.
2. Shut the instant pot with the pressure cooker lid, select the "pressure cook" option, select the high pressure setting
3. press +/- buttons to adjust the cooking time to 5 minutes, and then press the start button.
4. When done, do a natural pressure release, open the instant pot and then stir butter into the rice pudding
5. Serve straight away.

Nutrition Value:

- Calories: 387
- Fat: 3
- Carbs: 82
- Protein: 7
- Fiber: 2 g

Conclusion

The Instant Pot Duo Crisp Air Fryer is a revolutionary, unique, and highly sophisticated piece of equipment that is worth a lot more than its price. With its multipurpose place in the kitchen, it can do all the things you want to do and more. There is no need to buy the extra-expensive equipment. Just like a cell phone absorbed functions of different devices, this Instant Pot Duo Crisp Air Fryer has absorbed all the functions of different appliances and can easily become a standard in everyone's home.

The pot comes with instructions on preparing commonly used ingredients in the device so you can make your recipes with ease. Labeled buttons, a smart program, and a bright display ensure that you are never confused while cooking Cook time is greatly reduced with no compromise on the plate.

You cook every day, so why not make the experience more interesting and exciting Just trying the instant pot, you will see how easy and delicious your life has become. Trying new things is a part of life, and you will surely regret not using this device at least once.

Impress your friends with complicated dishes which you secretly make within minutes, set up a timer for always to have hot meals even when you are not around, and never again burn or overcook your food. Start using the Instant Pot Duo Crisp Air Fryer today and feel the change.

CPSIA information can be obtained
at www.ICGtesting.com
Printed in the USA
LVHW020149121220
674003LV00009B/349